Discover The
Mentally STRONG Method

A Personal Development Guidebook to help you think, organize, and choose in your journey of mental strength.

Dr. Cristi Bundukamara, Ed. D PMHNP

Author: Cristi Bundukamara, Ed.D, PMHNP

ISBN: 9798985650809

www.mentallystrong.com

Our Mission

To inspire all humanity to embrace the journey of mental strength.

"Don't silence your passion, you may just change the world."

~ Dr. B

To the new you,

I start this letter with the new you, because I believe the Mentally STRONG Method will allow you to become the best and most confident version of yourself. Now, approaching 50 years old, I can confidently say I love myself and have learned to be proud of my emotions and in control of them. I am Mentally STRONG, not because I was born that way, but because I learned to THINK, ORGANIZE, and CHOOSE.

I created the Mentally STRONG Method because I truly believe we can strengthen our brains. Mental strength is an attribute we admire in people; however, we do not teach it in any standard curriculum. This method is scientifically backed by cognitive behavioral theories and empowers you to gain insight, resilience, and mental strength on your lifetime journey of self-improvement.

Throughout this guidebook, you will find Choice Opportunity worksheets specially designed to assist you in working through specific aspects of yourself. You will also find places and opportunities for journaling or note writing to help you learn and process this formula.

I am looking forward to going with you on your journey for mental strength.

~ Dr. B

Table of Contents

Section 1

Who is Dr. B?

Introduction of Dr. Cristi Bundukamara

My name is Dr. Cristi Bundukamara and many call me Dr. B. I am a Psychiatric Mental Health Nurse Practitioner (PMHNP-BC), a Doctor of Healthcare Education (Ed. D), a daughter, a sister, a wife, a mother, and a friend. I have been through unimaginable trials in my life and have experienced many feelings as a result: depression, anxiety, anger, and overwhelming stress. After taking control of my thoughts and choices, however, I can confidently say, "I am now Mentally STRONG." Through the Power of Choice, I have chosen to feel happiness, love, joy, and hope.

After creating and using the Mentally STRONG Method on myself, I know that it works! And I know that I need to share it with you. This formula has helped me tremendously with coping, understanding, and thriving in my life, allowing me to be in a place where I can be Mentally STRONG.

If you are lost, feeling overwhelmed, or literally feeling anything at all, using The Mentally STRONG Method will help you. You can leverage it to map your thoughts, identify behaviors and choices, see connections to other areas of your life, and make sense of all of the randomness that seems to surround you. This process will allow you to identify what is blocking your progress, and the Mentally STRONG Method will empower you to take action. Often, we are paralyzed by our emotions, internal thinking, fear, and grief, but we don't need to stay that way. The Mentally STRONG Method provides a simple, extremely effective way to help change your life through the creation of a well-defined Personal Vision. You have control. The Mentally STRONG Method will help you to help yourself.

Dr. B's Journey

Many people say that I am the strongest person they know. Although I appreciate the encouraging words, what I really want others to understand is that I was not born this way. I have learned how to find strength, and I continually CHOOSE to find that strength every single day.

I was born to a very young mother who would not have described herself as strong. My father died when I was only 10 months old, and my mother had to rely on my grandmother to help raise me. We considered ourselves poor, a mostly dysfunctional, but loving family. Since I was as young as I can remember, I believed I was ugly, fat and not smart. By the time I was a teenager, I was angry, depressed, rebellious and had acquired an eating disorder, too.

My first boyfriend was emotionally and physically abusive. I spiraled downwards, had an abortion, and started using cocaine. I continued to make choices that I was not proud of, and eventually, the pressure to stay within the Army's weight standards led to a full-blown eating disorder for me.

In my early 20's, I learned cognitive behavioral therapy and started using it on myself to change my thoughts. I've watched my life transform since then. I know that people are giving me a compliment when they say that I am the strongest person they know, but the biggest compliment would be if they learned from my journey and chose to be Mentally STRONG.

In 2018, I authored a biography detailing my family's journey: "*Mentally STRONG: Against All Odds We Choose.*" To fully understand the depths of our challenges, I recommend that you read it. It documents my own struggles and family setbacks as well as my path to becoming Mentally STRONG as a choice. These personal experiences have had a huge influence on me and have been a driving force for the development of The Mentally STRONG Method and what it is today: a formula for mental strength.

I am also the mother of seven amazing children. Although I've been blessed with a beautiful family, my story turned abruptly from fairy tale to tragedy. It all began when I met the love of my life and watched with delight as our family grew in the form of biological and adopted children. But the bliss was short-lived as tragedy after tragedy began to strike our family: an accidental death, runaway teens, drug use and abuse, prostitution, and a devastating life-changing medical diagnosis impacting multiple family members. As you can probably imagine, it has often been overwhelming, challenging, and downright painful. Yet, against all odds, my family and I chose to fight, and we are still fighting today. We have decided to never give up, to choose strength and to find joy no matter what.

How I Developed the Mentally STRONG Method

I was at my desk one day, head in hands, crying. "I can't do this anymore. It's just too much," I whimpered. Every thought in my mind was bouncing around all of the decisions that needed to be made. What is best for my children? What should I do, stop the medication, or increase it? Did someone let the dog out? Should I try a new therapy? Should I move my daughter to a different school?

I felt like there were a million choices to be made at that exact moment. Important decisions, the outcomes of which were all dependent on me. I began to shut down with decision fatigue: I was becoming ineffective and overwhelmed with all of my thoughts. The chaos of life swirled around me, and I found it difficult to make both simple decisions and important choices for myself and those I loved.

My breakthrough came when I least expected it- at a point when I was spiraling. Like many of us do when we are at our wit's end, I reached out to my mom. Her seemingly simple advice led to my saving grace. "You should start a journal," she said, "it has really helped me tremendously to get my thoughts and feelings down on paper." I didn't think much of it at first but humored her by sitting down with a blank piece of paper and pen. As I stared at the empty page, for once, nothing came to mind. I had no thoughts to write down. Just crickets in my head. White noise.

In that moment, I realized that I didn't think in complete sentences, and concluded that, as such, journaling would take too much of my precious mental energy. I also knew from my professional experience as a psychiatric nurse practitioner that journaling can be unorganized and contain multiple random intrusive thoughts, a process that would not be supportive of the decision-making I wanted to complete.

Discouraged but not defeated, I decided to scribble out what I was thinking on that blank sheet of paper. Just words. Words everywhere spilling onto the page along with my tears. When I took a step back to look at what I had written, I noticed connections. I started to draw lines from one word to another marking those associations. It was almost like a game to connect the dots from word to word. It took me about twenty minutes, but it felt more like twenty years of journaling on that one piece of paper. I was able to organize my thoughts for the first time and consider the decisions that I faced while laying out a plan to act. I was blown away!

Now, 10 years later, the Mentally STRONG Method is a solid formula that has been used to help hundreds of other people, and I want to share it with you.

Section 2

Introduction to The Mentally STRONG Method

What is The Mentally STRONG Method?

The Mentally STRONG Method is a simple and practical method for developing mental strength. This empowering approach utilizes evidence-based research as its foundation in the form of cognitive- behavioral therapy. Cognitive-behavioral therapy (CBT) has been widely used as a primary treatment that emphasizes choice in association with principals of mental and behavioral change (Beck, 2011; Lefebvre, 1981), resulting in real physical changes in your brain. Brain imaging studies using functional magnetic resonance imaging (fMRI) have actually demonstrated CBT's ability to rewire whole areas of the brain, blood flow and neuronal activation (Duval et al. 2015). These results are incredible and demonstrate that we all have the power to learn this method and change the way that we think.

I challenge you to embark on the process of learning the Mentally STRONG Method and taking responsibility for your own mental health. With the use of the Mentally STRONG Method on your personal journey, you will be supported to achieve a healthy mental state so that you can overcome issues, conflicts, and process thoughts. This method will allow you to deal with both significant concerns as well as lesser daily struggles. Becoming mentally strong is a life-long, learning journey. You will be constantly evolving and changing with it as you grow.

When you become fluent with the process, you will map your thoughts in relation to your past (your story), identify and organize those thoughts, and then embrace your power to choose. Afterwards, armed with insight, you will be empowered to move forward toward a meaningful Personal Vision for yourself. The Mentally STRONG Method provides an opportunity for you to develop while helping yourself and others.

The Mentally STRONG Method consists of four elements which we will describe in detail throughout this workbook. The process can be further simplified into three main concepts, or words: THINK, ORGANIZE, and CHOOSE. Here is a brief description of each of the four elements:

Element 1: The Thought Map

A Thought Map is a visual activity which will enable you to identify a central thought or feeling that you are experiencing or struggling with. On a worksheet, you will list this central thought or feeling along with the contributing factors tied to it. The purpose of the Thought Map is to help you gain insight into how your past thoughts and experiences are impacting your current thought processes. This involves THINKING without rumination. It can become comfortable to focus on our current problems, but the reality is that many dysfunctional thought patterns started in early childhood and are still evident in the many similar thoughts and feelings we experience today.

Element 2: Identify and Organize

In this element, you will pinpoint the important factors contributing to the identified central thought in your Thought Map and organize them into ten categories. The purpose of the identify and organize element is to learn how to ORGANIZE your thoughts.

Element 3: Power of Choice

In this element, you will identify where change is possible or desired in each category. Then, you will have the opportunity to decide how you can go about making those changes. I encourage you to use your Choice Opportunity Worksheets to assist you in processing and planning those choices (these worksheets are placed throughout this workbook).

The purpose of the Power of Choice section is more than just to CHOOSE. Its purpose is to be able to make those choices in organized categories. Many proponents of positive psychology will often say that you should just choose to think positive. This is both true and false. It is true that positive thinking will help reverse and rewire your negative thoughts, but it's also false because it won't help with your grief and trauma. Therefore, it's important to work through the items in each category differently.

Element 4: Personal Vision:

In this element, you will develop several empowering Personal Visions for multiple areas of your life so that you can achieve sustainable, healthy mental strength. The purpose of creating your Personal Vision is to help drive your CHOICES *now*. You want to make sure your decisions today are in line with what you want in your life and the kind of person that you want to become.

Are you ready?

As preparation for kickstarting your journey for improving your life by using the Mentally STRONG Method, I have included three activities in this section to help you get started. The first is The Mentally STRONG Scale, the second is the "Feelings Log," and the third is "Developing your Personal Vision." As part of these initial activities, start to really notice how you are thinking and feeling during the day and begin to brainstorm about what you want your Personal Vision to be.

The image on the next page is a visual representation of the four elements. The Personal Vision element is like an umbrella over the other elements. For this reason, we encourage you to start thinking first about what your Personal Visions are for yourself. You will continually refer to these Personal Visions when working through the other elements: the Thought Map, Identify & Organize and especially the Power of Choice found within The Mentally Strong Method.

As you embark on the Mentally STRONG method, you will learn it by going through the elements starting with Element 1 and ending with Element 4. The reality is, after you have mastered the method, it is a fluid process of THINK (ing), ORGANIZE (ing) and CHOOSE (ing). You can move in and out of working in any Element at any time and in any order. Some may find it helpful to follow all the instructions in order each time. The purpose is for you to always be working towards your Personal Visions. The umbrella over the process is to remind you to continue to call upon your Personal Vision as you work through the method.

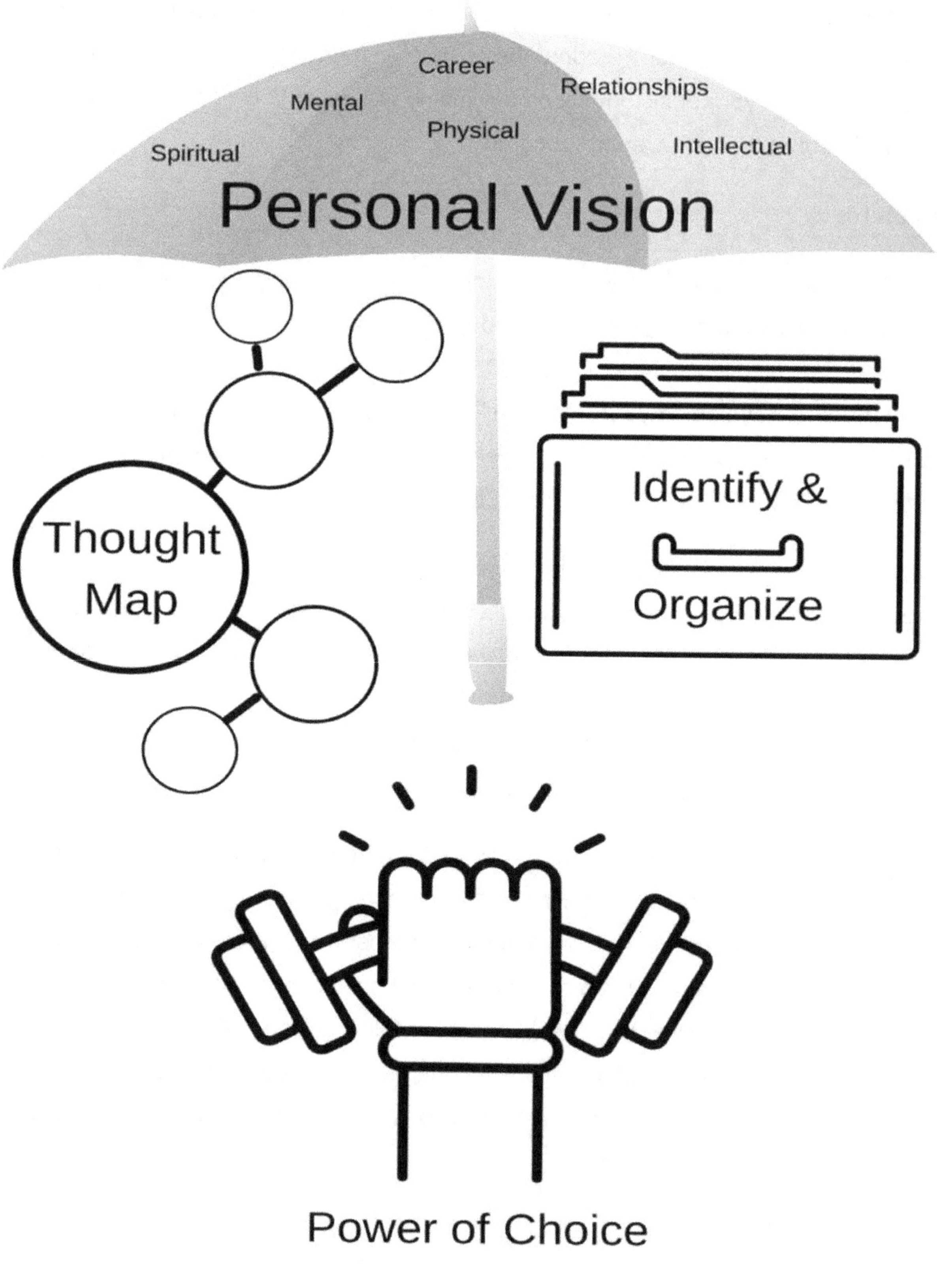

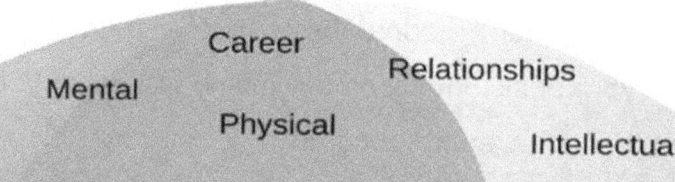

Career

Mental

Relationships

Physical

Spiritual

Intellectual

Personal Vision

Thought Map

Identify & Organize

Power of Choice

The Mentally STRONG Scale

The Mentally STRONG scale was developed after 15 years of my own personal use of the Mentally STRONG method and 3 years of professional implementation with clients in the Mentally STRONG Medical Model. The scale is based on the four elements of the method and showcases how learning this cognitive behavioral approach improves your ability to handle stress, overcome obstacles and feel confident.

It's your turn to begin. You will find a blank scale on the next page. Please fill it out now before continuing on in this book, so that you will be able to compare your progress after learning and using the Mentally STRONG Method on yourself.

Upon creating the scale, I completed it for myself. After you fill out your own scale, you will see mine. The black dot is what I would have answered before using cognitive behavioral (thought-changing) techniques on myself and the heart is where I see myself today. Although I am not "very confident" in all areas, I am confident most of the time. It is very important for me to admit that I have been working on my mental health with cognitive behavioral methods since my early 20's. Now, I no longer have an eating disorder, I manage my depression, I am not addicted to any substance, and I am proud of myself and my choices. That is the outcome of 20 plus years of genuine, insightful, hard work.

On the next page, fill out the Mentally STRONG Scale for yourself according to how you are feeling right now.

Mentally STRONG Scale

How confident are you that you can think through your problems/issues, organize your thoughts, and make decisions that you are proud of?

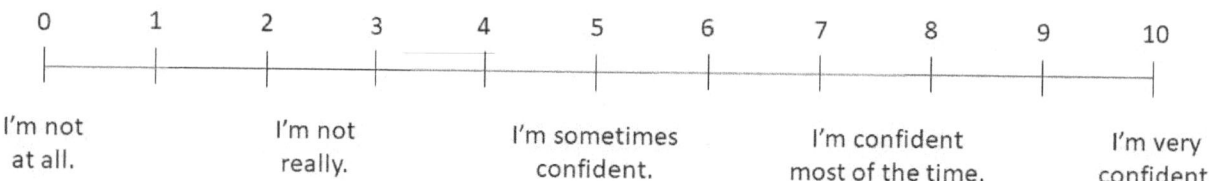

How confident are you that you have insight into your past and how it impacts your thoughts and mood today?

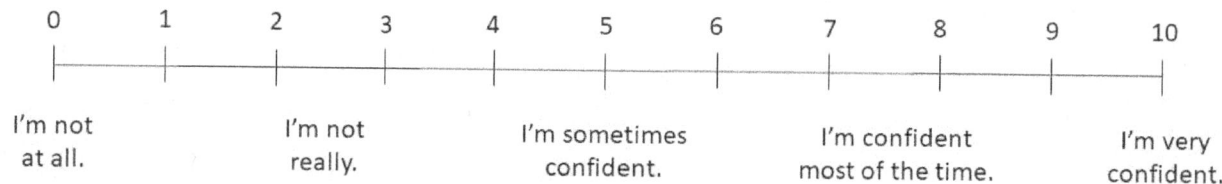

How confident are you that you can manage your triggers so that they don't impact your thoughts and/or mood?

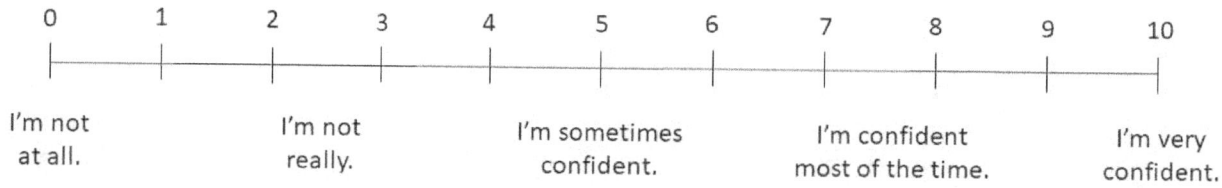

How confident are you that you have processed grief in your life?

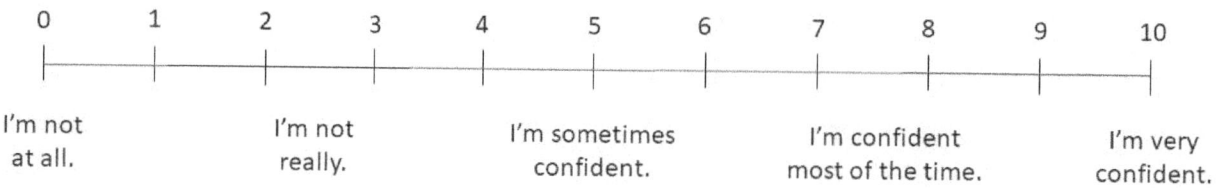

How confident are you that you have processed your trauma and can manage the impact trauma has had on your life? If you have never experienced trauma, circle 10. This is a protective factor that you can be grateful for.

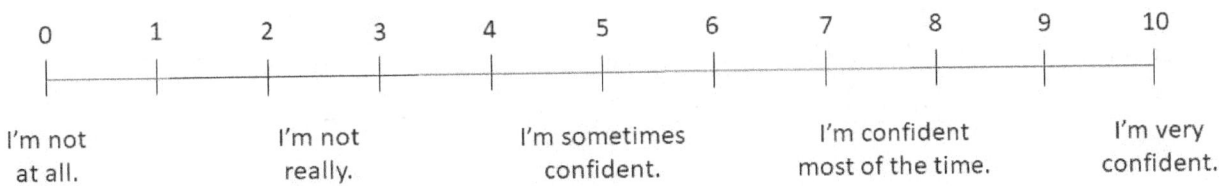

How confident are you that you can consistently reframe your negative thoughts into realistic positive thoughts?

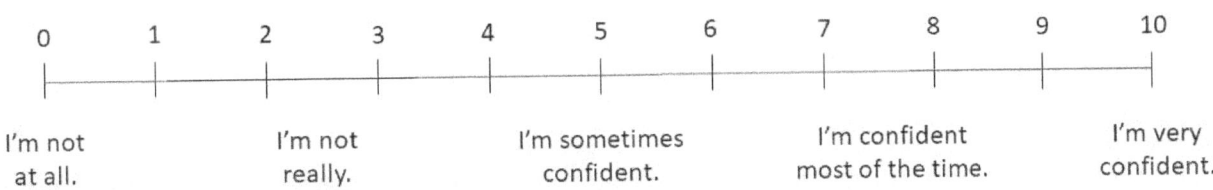

How confident are you that you have insight into how past decisions are currently impacting your thoughts, mood, and life?

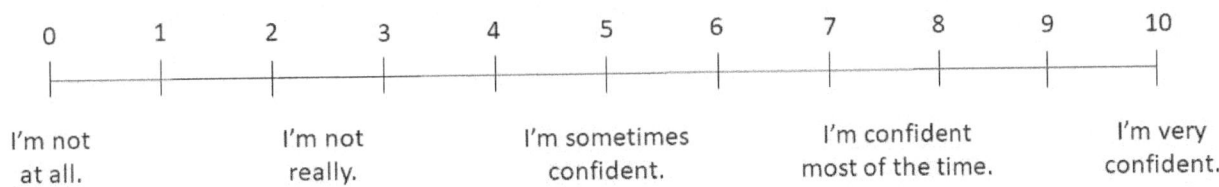

How confident are you in your ability to change behaviors that have a negative impact on you?

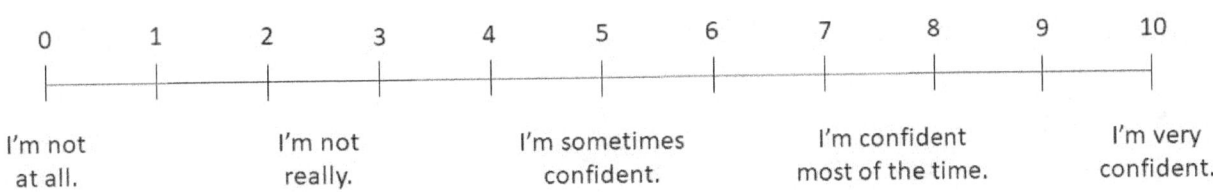

Are you confident in your ability to manage your anxiety, worry or fear?

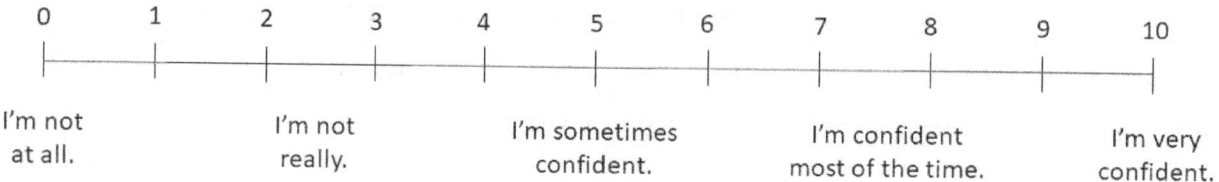

How confident are you that you can think, organize those thoughts, and choose a productive response when you experience or witness an injustice?

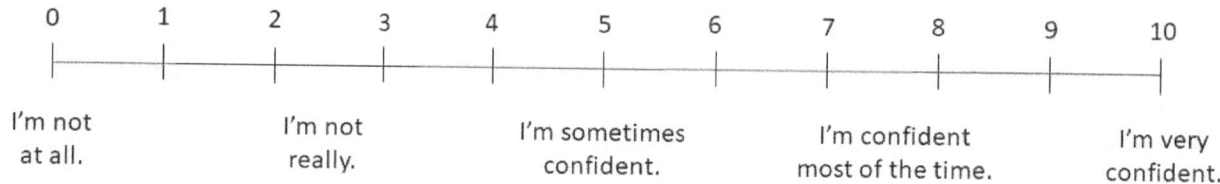

How confident are you in managing how injustices impact your thoughts and mood?

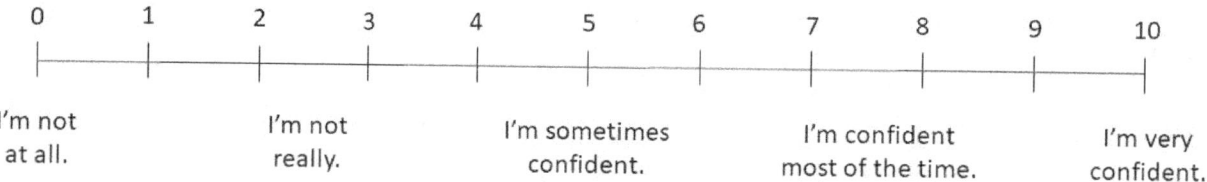

How confident are you in your spiritual relationship or belief system that improves your quality of life?

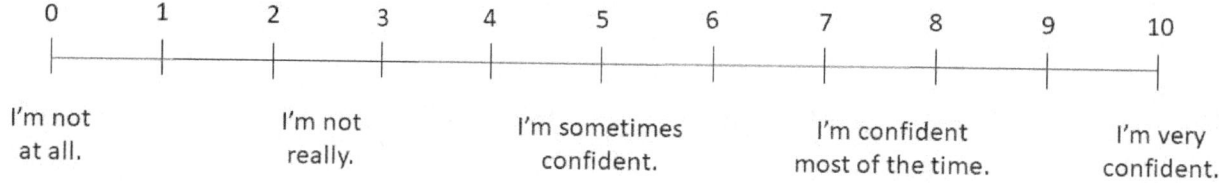

How confident are you that you can manage your addiction? If you have never experienced addiction, circle 10. This is a protective factor that you can be grateful for.

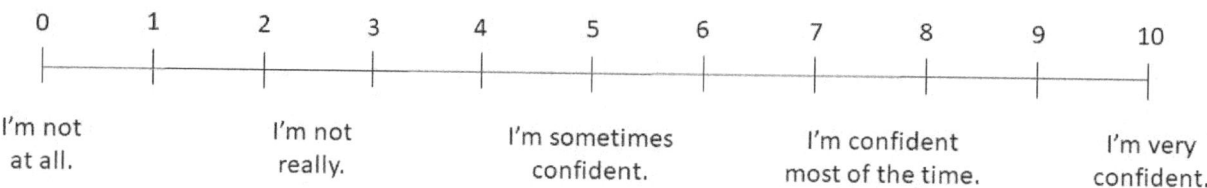

How confident are you in your ability to make healthy choices in line with what you want in your life?

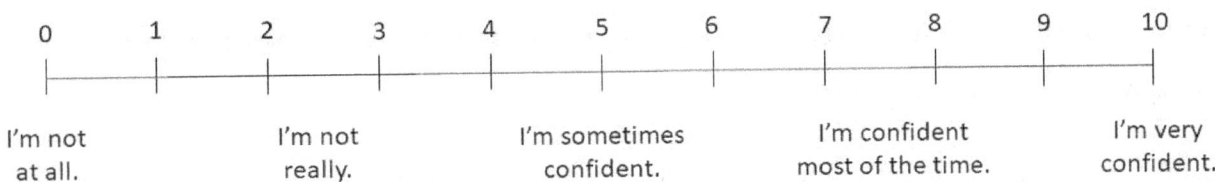

How confident are you in your ability to make meaningful choices in line with what you want in your relationships?

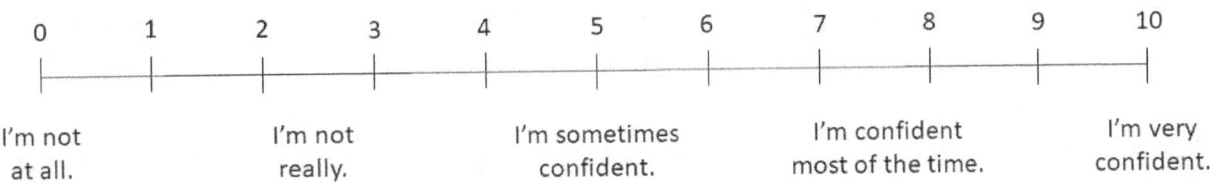

How confident are you in your ability to make productive choices in line with what you want in your work or career?

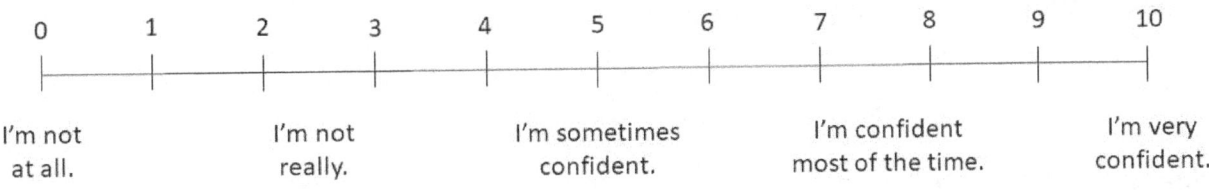

How confident are you in your mental strength to manage expectations of your work life balance?

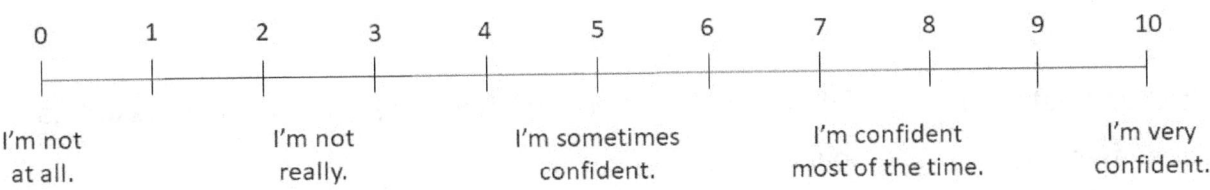

Mentally STRONG Scale Interpretation

Add up all your points.

0-35 – You may be overly critical of yourself, or you know that you really need to work on your confidence in your ability to organize your thoughts and make choices that are in line with your Personal Visions.

36-65 - You know that you really need to work on your confidence in your ability to organize your thoughts and make choices that are in line with your Personal Visions. You can do this!

66-105 – You are insightful and understand that sometimes you are confident and sometimes you are not. This is a great place to start. Everyone can use improvement!

106-140 - You are very confident in your ability to organize your thoughts; The Mentally STRONG Method can definitely help you improve even more!

141-170 – You are already well on your way to being able to organize your thoughts and make choices that are in line with your Personal Visions. If you had a perfect score though, I urge to look a little deeper. None of us are perfect and you may need to gain some insight into your thoughts and feelings.

What was your score? _____

Did you think that the scale is accurate? _____

Where would you like to be? _____

When you get to the end of this guidebook, you will have the opportunity to take this assessment again to see how far you have come!

My Personal Scale

The following is the scale that I filled out. The black dot is what I would have answered before using cognitive behavioral thought changing techniques on myself and the heart is where I see myself today.

Dr. B's Mentally STRONG Scale

How confident are you that you can think through your problems/issues, organize your thoughts, and make decisions that you are proud of?

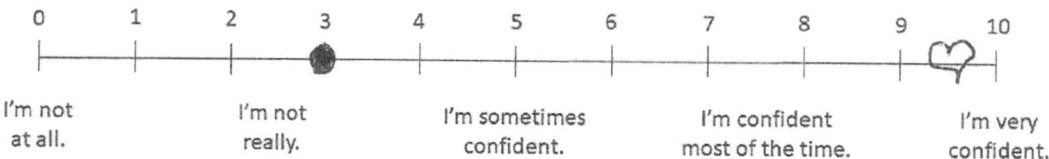

How confident are you that you have insight into your past and how it impacts your thoughts and mood today?

How confident are you that you can manage your triggers, where they don't impact your thoughts and/or mood?

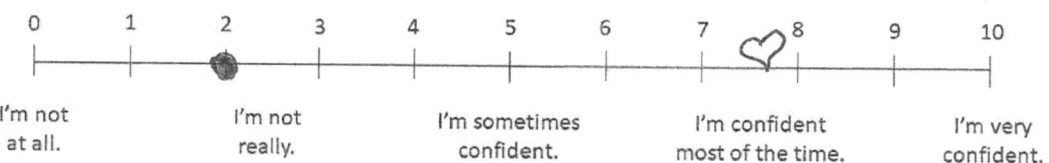

How confident are you that you have processed grief in your life?

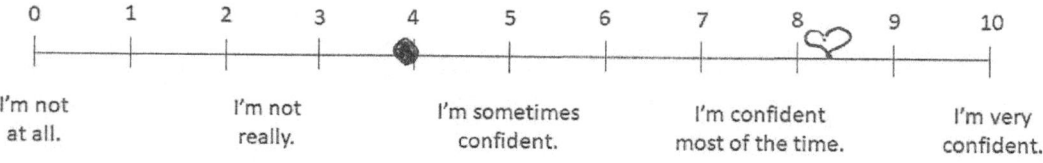

How confident are you that you have processed your trauma and can manage the impact trauma has had on your life? If you have never experienced trauma, circle 10, this is a protective factor that you can be grateful for.

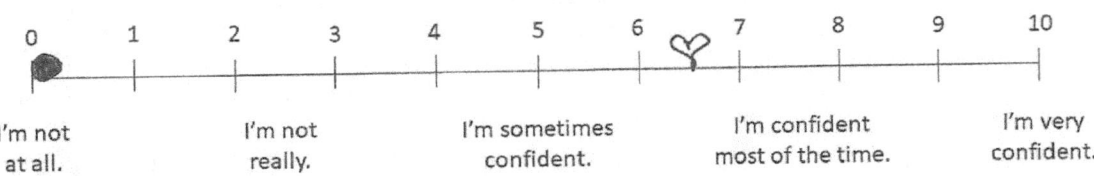

How confident are you that you can consistently reframe your negative thoughts into realistic positive thoughts?

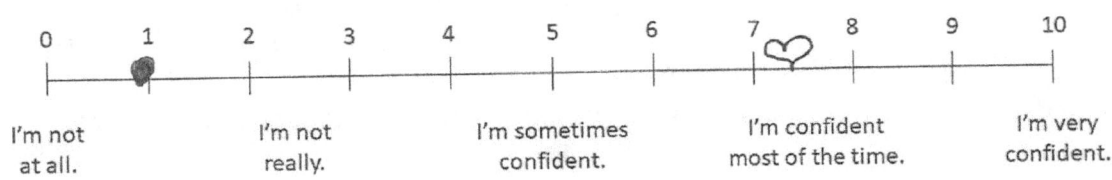

How confident are you that you have insight into how past decisions are currently impacting your thoughts, mood, and life?

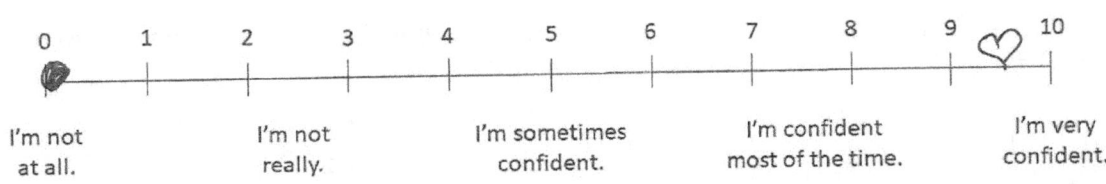

How confident are you in your ability to change behaviors that have a negative impact on you?

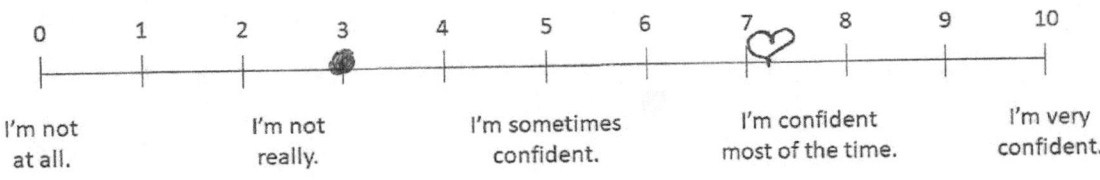

Are you confident in your ability to manage your anxiety, worry or fear?

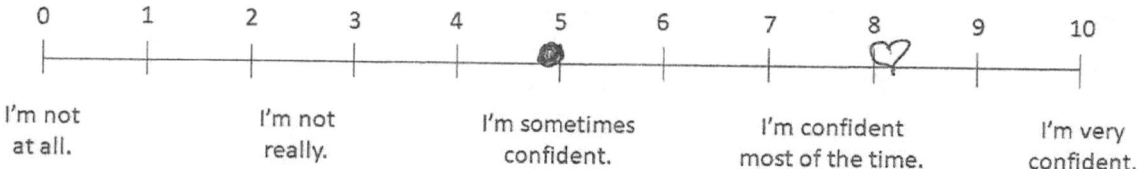

How confident are you that you can think, organize, and choose a reaction that you can be proud of when you experience or witness an injustice?

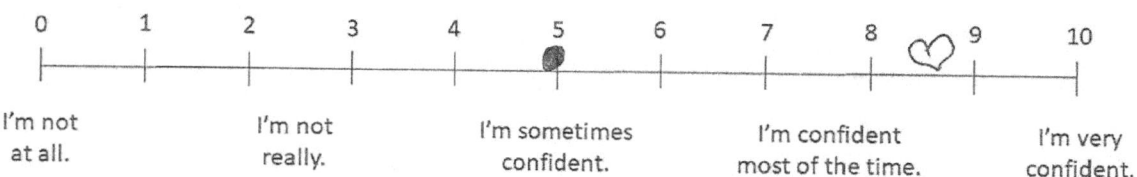

How confident are you in managing how injustices impact your thoughts and mood?

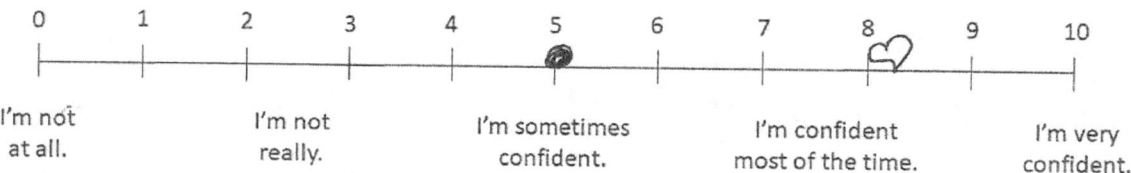

How confident are you in your spiritual relationship or belief system that improves your quality of life?

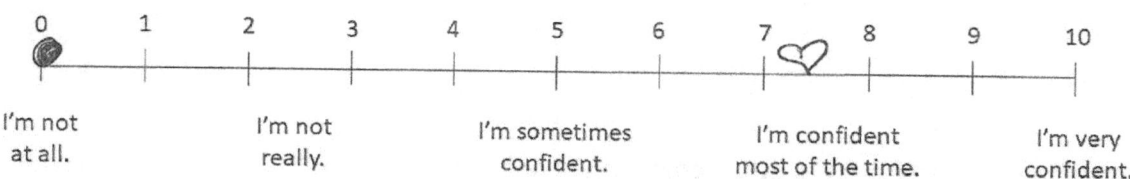

How confident are you that you can manage your addiction? If you have never experienced addiction, circle 10, this is a protective factor that you can be grateful for.

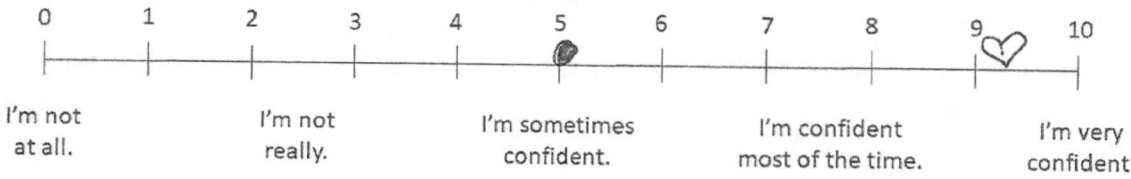

How confident are you in your ability to make healthy choices in line with what you want in your life?

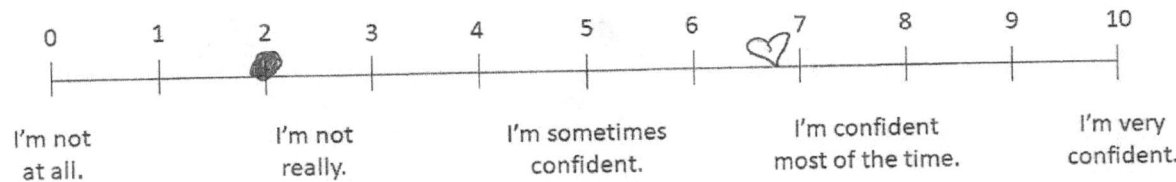

How confident are you in your ability to make meaningful choices in line with what you want in your relationships?

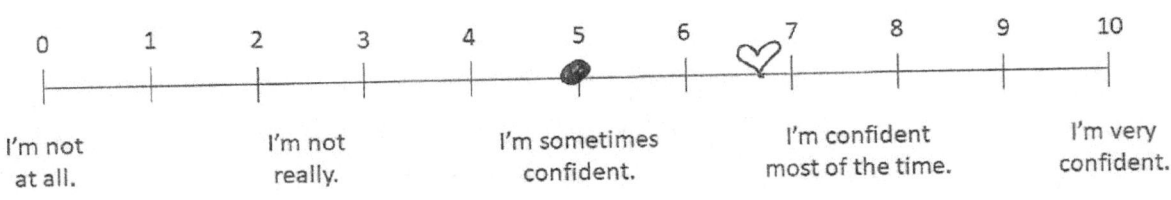

How confident are you in your ability to make productive choices in line with what you want in your work or career?

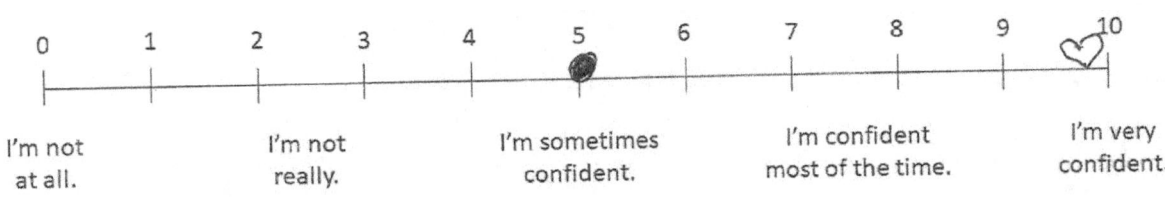

How confident are you in your mental strength to manage expectations of your work life balance?

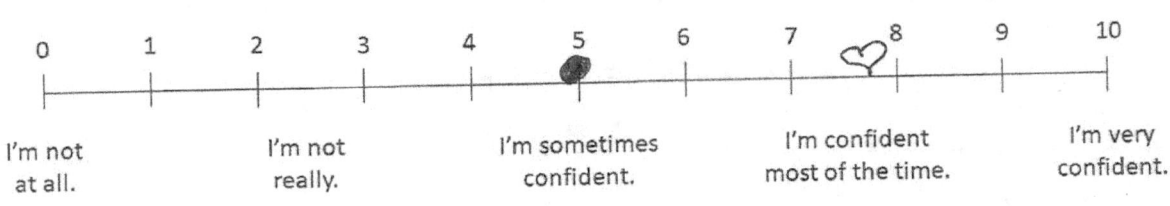

"Insight = Confidence" – *Dr. B*

How are you feeling before you start to learn the Mentally Strong Method? What to you hope to change and achieve? Do you have any fears or concerns?

_____

_____

_____

_____

_____

_____

_____

_____

_____

_____

_____

_____

_____

_____

_____

_____

Choice Opportunities

What are Choice Opportunities? Choice Opportunities are worksheets that help you make choices in the THINK, ORGANIZE and CHOOSE process of the Mentally STRONG method. There are Choice Opportunities that align with each category in this workbook. Typically, however, Choice Opportunities are used in the categories of element three, the Power of Choice, to help you dig deeper regarding your choices.

In this workbook, Choice Opportunities are presented throughout starting with the Feelings Log to help you identify feelings before learning element one, the Thought Map. After that, there is a Choice Opportunity on developing your Personal Vision. Remember that your Personal Vision is the umbrella over the other Elements of the Mentally STRONG Method so give it the attention that it deserves.

Activity Time!

It's time for you to complete the Feelings Log. The Feelings Log is designed to help you gain insight into the feelings that you have throughout the day. Using this log, you'll note the range of feelings that you are experiencing, and it will guide you into deeper understanding of those feelings. Choose to complete this Choice Opportunity Worksheet at least three times per day at first.

Choice Opportunity: Feelings Log

Expected outcome: Gain insight into a variety of your feelings by recording them. This log will help you see the range of feelings you are experiencing and will help guide you in understanding and really feeling them in order to grow towards mental strength.

INSTRUCTIONS: Choose to complete this Choice Opportunity at least 3 times per day and when you experience a new feeling and answer the questions in the spaces for that date and time.

Date Time of Day	Emotion You Felt	Rating at that moment: (0-10 scale) 0=None 10= Worst	Reflect and ponder the questions above about the feeling felt.	Insight Questions
		/10 *Depression /10 *Anxiety /10 *Overall Stress		New Feeling yes/ no Pleasant / Unpleasant Trigger yes / no Reoccuring yes / no
		/10 *Depression /10 *Anxiety /10 *Overall Stress		New Feeling yes/ no Pleasant / Unpleasant Trigger yes / no Reoccuring yes / no
		/10 *Depression /10 *Anxiety /10 *Overall Stress		New Feeling yes/ no Pleasant / Unpleasant Trigger yes / no Reoccuring yes / no
		/10 *Depression /10 *Anxiety /10 *Overall Stress		New Feeling yes/ no Pleasant / Unpleasant Trigger yes / no Reoccuring yes / no
		/10 *Depression /10 *Anxiety /10 *Overall Stress		New Feeling yes/ no Pleasant / Unpleasant Trigger yes / no Reoccuring yes / no
		/10 *Depression /10 *Anxiety /10 *Overall Stress		New Feeling yes/ no Pleasant / Unpleasant Trigger yes / no Reoccuring yes / no

The Mentally STRONG Method
1-800-55-STRONG www.mentallyvstrong.com

Author: Cristi Bundukamara

ABC List of Feelings! To Get You Started. You are NOT limited to this list of feelings.

Aggravated, Accepted, Alienated, Amazed, Amused, Angry, Annoyed, Anxious, Apathetic, Ashamed, Awful

Blah, Blissful, Bored

Calm, Chaotic, Cheerful, Confident, Confused, Content, Corgaeous, Cranky, Crazy, Critical, Crushed, Curious, Cynical

Defensive, Depressed, Determined, Devestated, Disappointed, Disillusioned, Drained

Eager, Ecstatic, Embarresed, Empty, Energetic, Envious, Excited, Exhausted, Empty

Fearful, Frustrated, Fulfilled

Grateful, Grief, Grumpy, Guilty

Happy, Heartbroken, Hopeful, Hurt

Ignored, Important, Inadequate, Indifferent, Inferior, Inspired, Irritaed

Jealous, Joyful

Lethargic, Listless, Lonely, Loved, Loving

Mellow, Micheivevious, Motivated

Naughty, Numb

Open, Optimistic, Overwhlemed

Peaceful, Pessimistic, Playful, Pleased, Powerful, Powerless, Proud

Refreshed, Rejected, Relaxed, Relieved, Restless

Sad, Satisfied, Scared, Sensitive, Skeptical, Shocked, Smart, Stressed, Surprised, Suspucious

Terrified, Threatened

Vulnerable

Worried, Wothless, Withdrawn

Examples of physical sensations: headache, heart ache, hot/cold, tremors, clear headed, lightness, stomach butterfiles, flutters, shallow breathing, jittery, heavy heart, stuffy nose, tension (i.e., neck, shoulders, jaw, lower back etc)

Challenge to Feel Feelings NOT on the List Above.

The Mentally STRONG Method
1-800-55-STRONG www.mentallystrong.com

Author: Cristi Bundukamara

Let's Keep Working!

You have already completed your scale and feelings log - go you! The last activity in this section is called "Developing your Personal Vision." Although your Personal Vision is the fourth element, you should start thinking about what you want your life to look like in specific areas so that you can make choices in line with what you really desire. Remember that your Personal Vision is the umbrella over all of the other elements so think about it long and hard. Once you have finished your Personal Vision, it will be time to actually start the Mentally Strong Method.

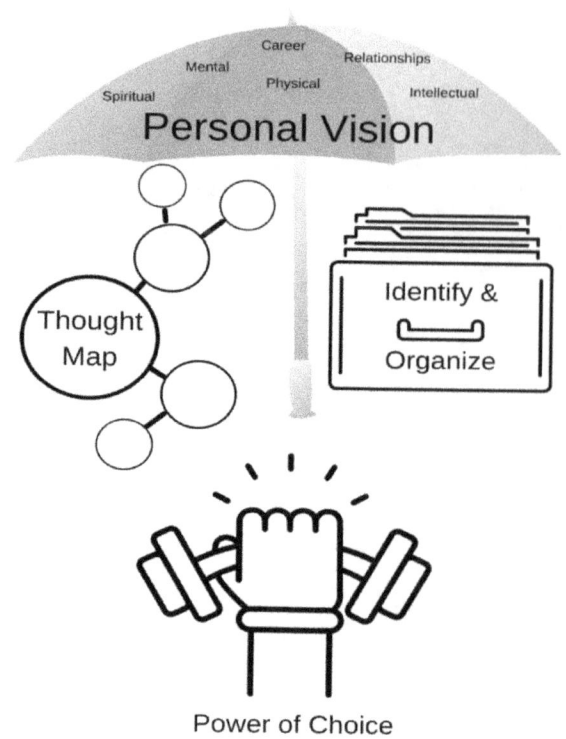

Power of Choice

Choice Opportunity: Developing Your Personal Vision

Expected Outcome: Start working on developing your personal visions. This is only the first step in the Personal Vision element.

Choose a category below and brainstorm ideas of what you want your Personal Vision to look like. This can change over time.

Physical ☐   Financial ☐   Intelligence ☐

Mental ☐   Career ☐   Lifestyle ☐

Emotional ☐   Purpose ☐   Sobriety ☐

Spiritual ☐   Relationships ☐   Other ☐

Faith ☐   Family ☐

My Personal Vision around _____:	My Personal Vision around _____:
My Personal Vision around _____:	My Personal Vision around _____:

Section 3

Element 1: The Thought Map

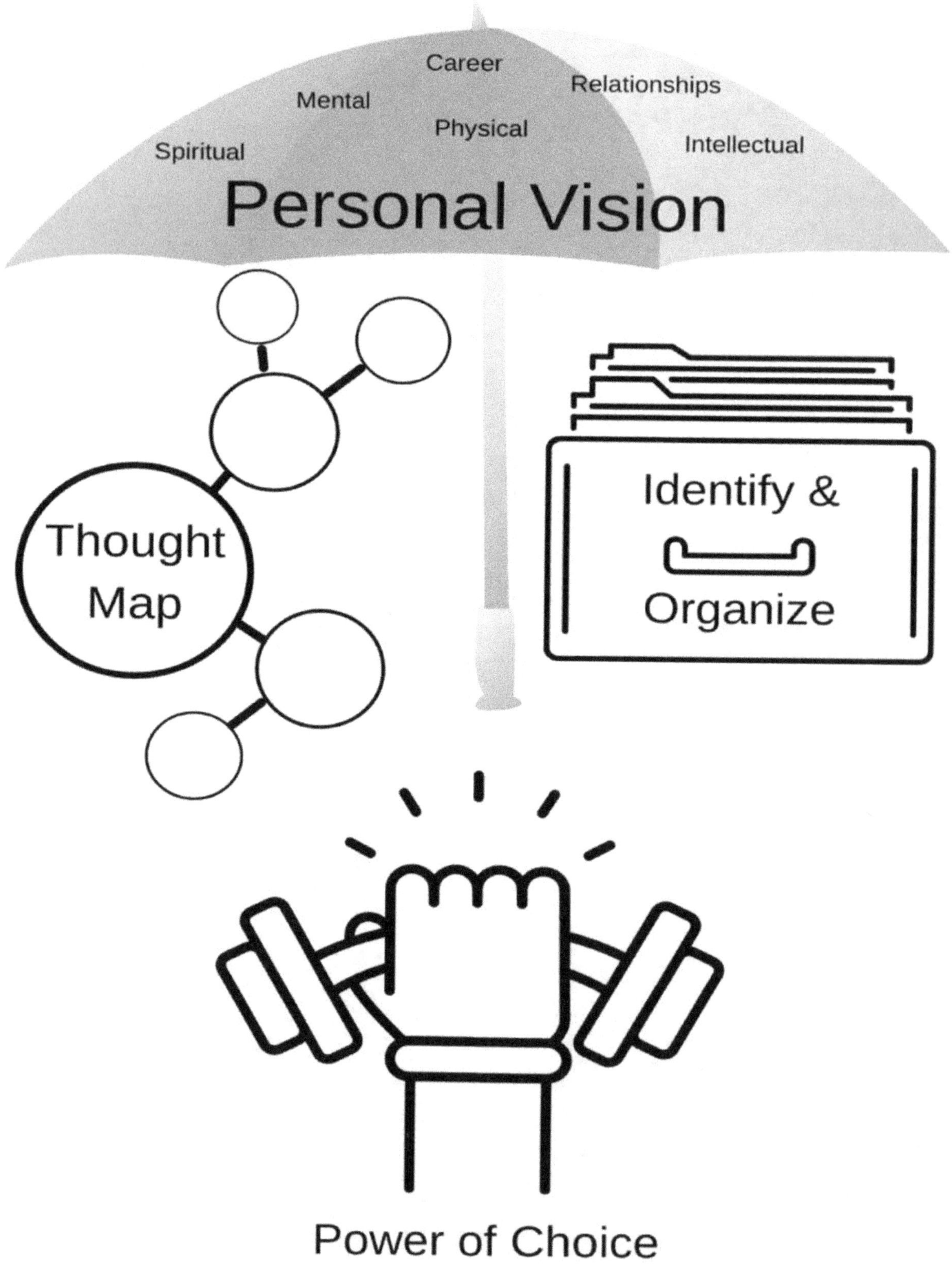

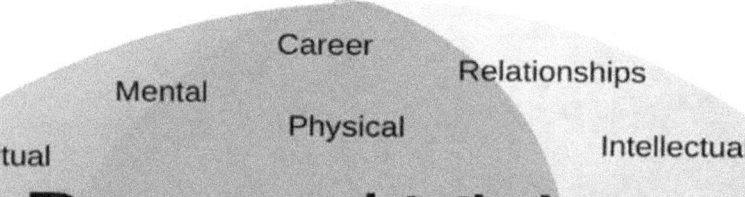

Career

Mental   Relationships

Physical

Spiritual   Intellectual

Personal Vision

Thought
Map

Identify &
Organize

Power of Choice

Element 1: The Thought Map

Hopefully, you've already completed your Personal Vision Choice Opportunity as it will set the tone for our work moving forward. Now, you are going to start your own journey to gain mental strength. Are you ready? It all begins with the Thought Map. The intention of the Thought Map is to give you greater insight into and control of your thoughts. Your goal when working on your Thought Map is to get the thoughts or feelings out and to explore all of the details that surround them. So, go back to your Feelings Log and choose a thought or feeling to get started.

On the Thought Map worksheet, use the following instructions to start writing down all of your stressors along with the thoughts and feelings that you are experiencing. When you are finished, look for patterns. You may begin to notice a theme and that one thought or feeling is more prevalent than others.

Once you have completed this first element, you will start to see those connections within your Thought Map. The Thought Map can be completed many times with any feeling or thought that you're experiencing. This is a critical activity as once it's been done; you will be ready to begin organizing your unhealthy thoughts and patterns. The Thought Map is your foundation, highlighting your underlying thoughts, feelings, and stressors. When you are ready to move into the remaining elements, you will do so with more insight and the ability to identify and organize your thoughts because you have put them out there and brainstormed about them.

Each of the components within the Thought Map are important and have a purpose. While learning the Mentally STRONG Method, you will identify the contributing factors related to your central thought or feeling. You might surprise yourself when you begin to notice the connections that you did not originally recognize; those which are currently impacting your choices and behaviors. Now, it's time to allow your thoughts and feelings to come alive on paper. This experience will be different for everyone, and you will have a fresh experience every time you do a Thought Map.

Central Thought

To get started on your first Thought Map, tear out or photocopy (for personal use) the blank Thought Map to the right and follow along with your map while moving through the following instructions and answering the questions:

What is the **CENTRAL THOUGHT or FEELING** that you are experiencing now, or the thought or feeling that you want to work through?

Write that thought (or feeling) in the largest circle in the center of your Thought Map. You may also refer back to your Feelings Log at this point.

Examples can include, but are not limited to:

- Anger
- Rage
- Stressed
- Inferior
- Violated
- Overwhelmed
- Upset
- Frustrated
- Anxious
- Fearful
- Disrespected

- Judged
- Inadequate
- Responsible
- Misunderstood
- Failure
- Unappreciated
- Grief
- Guilty
- Skeptical
- And so many other thoughts/feelings possible

Use this spot to journal about how you've come to this feeling or conclusion and reflect upon this central thought or feeling.

_____

_____

_____

My First Thought Map
(Tear me out or copy me)

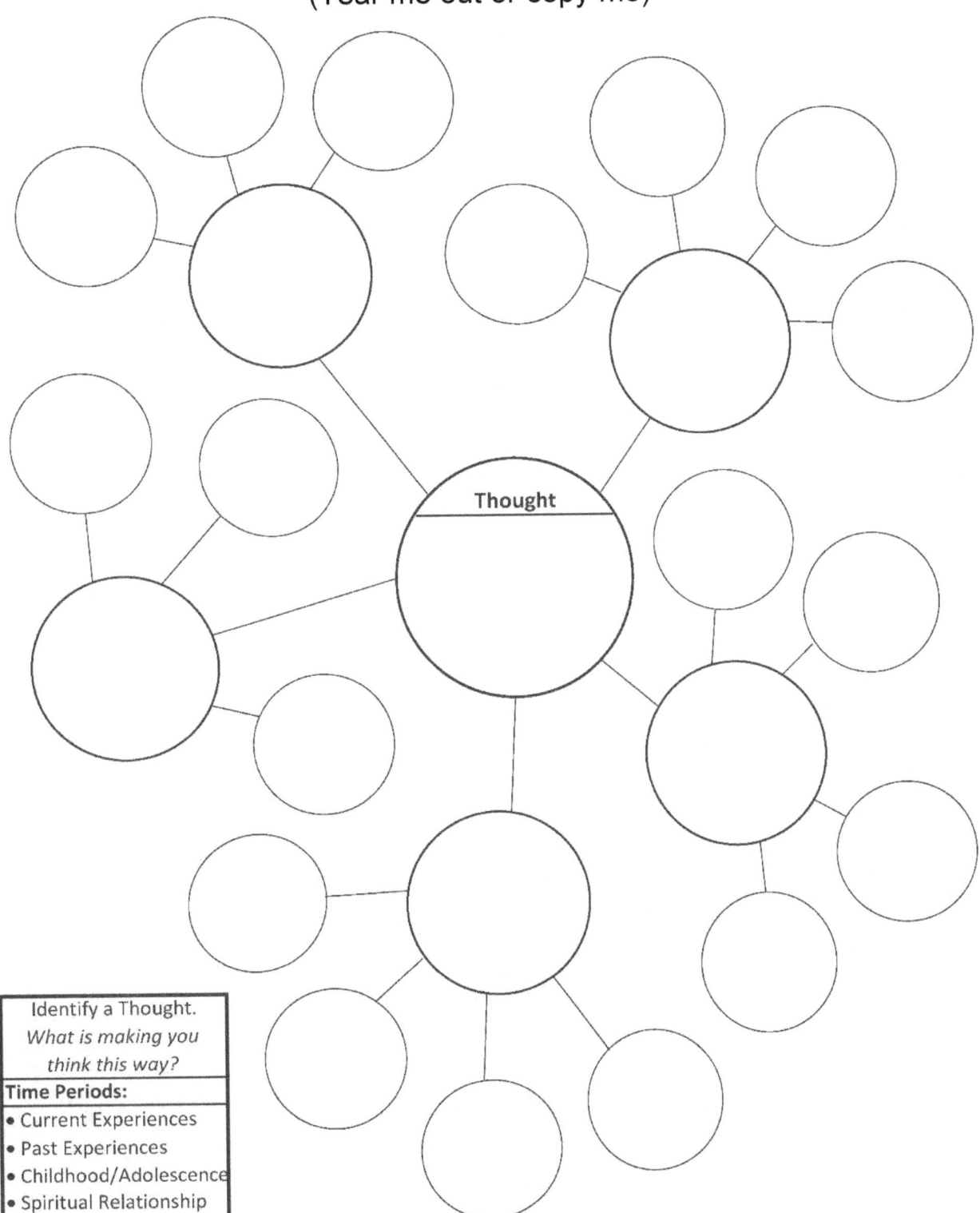

Thought

Identify a Thought.
What is making you think this way?

Time Periods:
- Current Experiences
- Past Experiences
- Childhood/Adolescence
- Spiritual Relationship

Now it's time to write down your central thought or feeling.

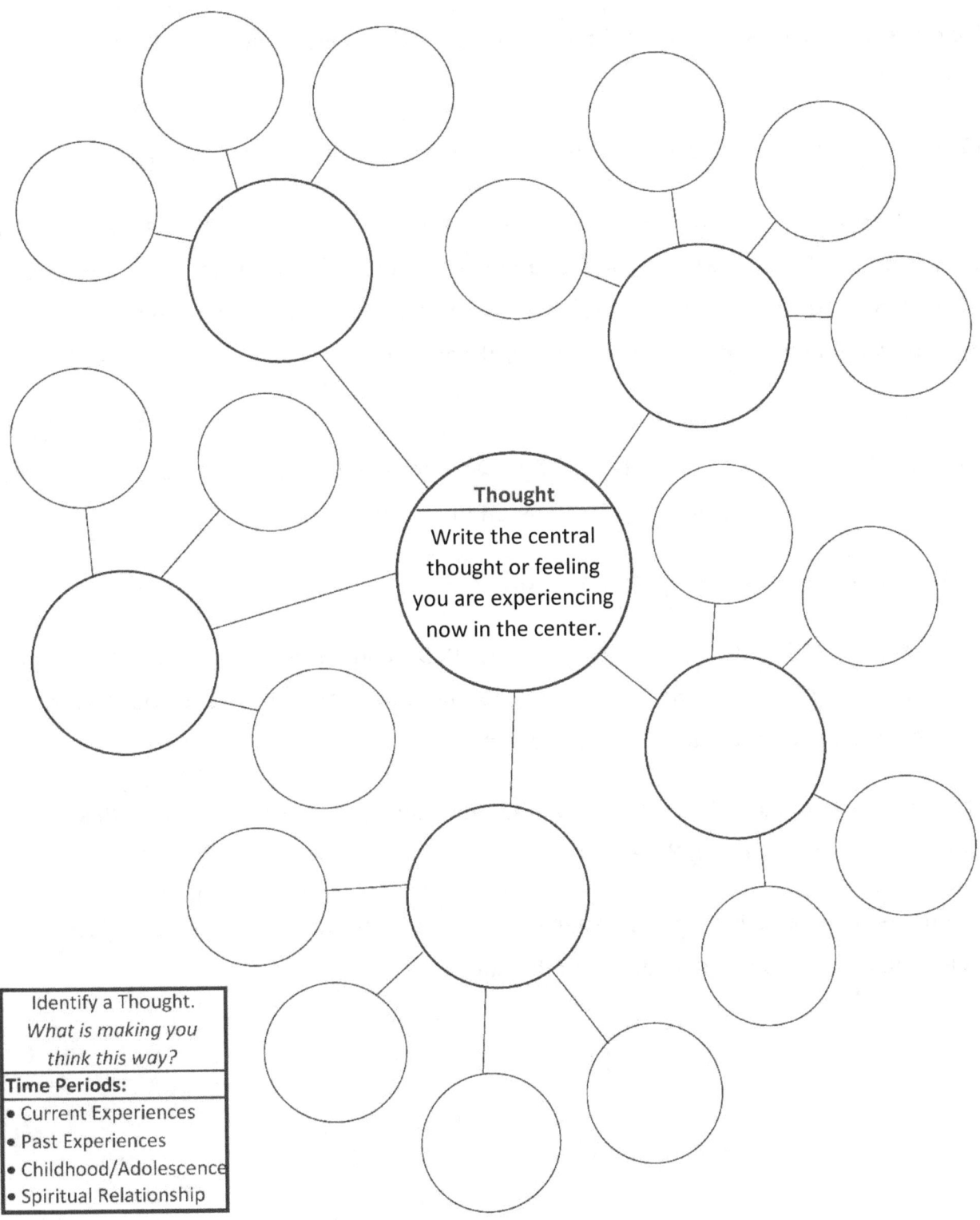

Thought

Write the central thought or feeling you are experiencing now in the center.

Identify a Thought.
What is making you think this way?

Time Periods:
- Current Experiences
- Past Experiences
- Childhood/Adolescence
- Spiritual Relationship

37

Current Influences

Now that your central thought or feeling has been identified, answer the following question:

What details are currently contributing to your central thought or feeling?

There is likely more than one person, thing, event, experience, or situation contributing to the central thought you identified in your Thought Map. Write them all down. Feel free to use as many circles as you need to in order to capture all of the contributing factors that are making you think this way.

While working in this area, remember to stay focused on *the central thought* that you identified. Other thoughts and feelings can come up with your Thought Map as you map out your experiences but try to focus on the main one.

In this step, you will keep going deeper.

Branch out by listing other factors and supporting details related to this thought. This space is one where you can drill down and uncover more layers associated with the factors that you are currently experiencing.

The main question to ask yourself is: *What other factors are associated with this identified thought or feeling?*

Examples of items to list include experiences, events, people, past trauma or losses, beliefs, and behaviors associated with the circles.

Now it's time to write down what is currently influencing your central thought.

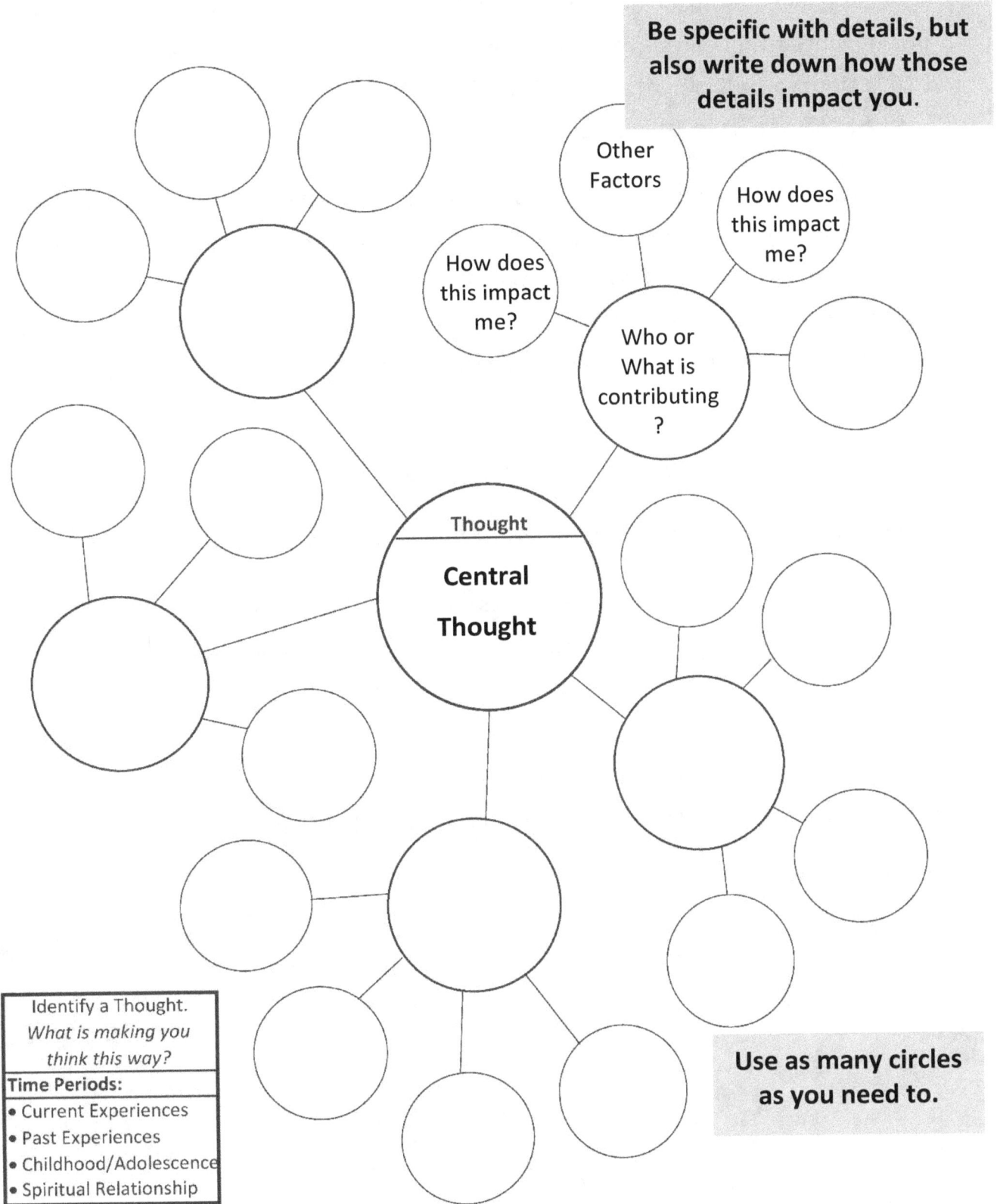

Be specific with details, but also write down how those details impact you.

Other Factors

How does this impact me?

How does this impact me?

Who or What is contributing?

Thought

Central Thought

Identify a Thought.
What is making you think this way?

Time Periods:
- Current Experiences
- Past Experiences
- Childhood/Adolescence
- Spiritual Relationship

Use as many circles as you need to.

Past Experiences

We all have a past, and our current thinking is influenced by our past. So, even though those experiences are not present in our lives today, they are still influencing us. In this step, you will identify the **PAST EXPERIENCES** associated with your central thought until you have listed all of these details.

Keep in mind that the purpose of going into the past is NOT to relive it, bring up old memories, or to open old wounds. It is simply to see how your past experiences influence your current thinking (and again, they do). Completing this step will allow you to see connections, themes, patterns or trends in behaviors and choices; they will be in relation to experiences, people, situations, events, beliefs, internal conflicts, past trauma, or losses.

When you are ready, answer the following question:

What has contributed to you thinking or feeling this way in the recent past?

On the worksheet, identify times in the past where you have also experienced this thought or feeling to uncover possible influences and document them.

Keep going deeper.

Reflect more. Continue listing other factors that have contributed to this thought or feeling in your past. You are likely to find many other instances.

Now it's time to write down factors that influenced your central thought in the past.

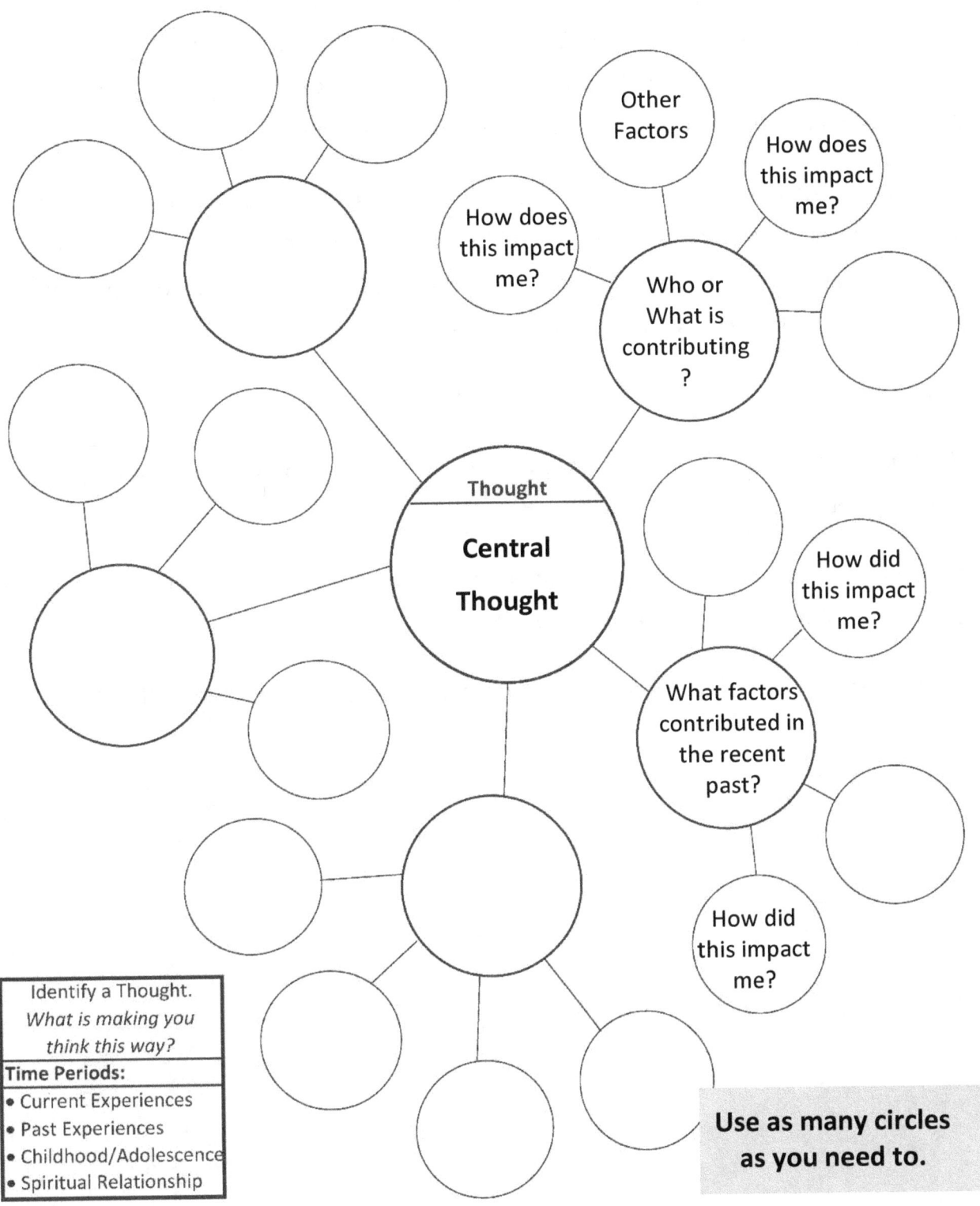

Other Factors

How does this impact me?

How does this impact me?

Who or What is contributing ?

Thought

Central Thought

How did this impact me?

What factors contributed in the recent past?

How did this impact me?

Identify a Thought.
What is making you think this way?
Time Periods:
• Current Experiences
• Past Experiences
• Childhood/Adolescence
• Spiritual Relationship

Use as many circles as you need to.

Childhood or Adolescence

As a fourth step, you are going to turn the clock way back. Identify times in your **CHILDHOOD AND ADOLESCENCE** that are associated with the identified thought that you are still experiencing today Once again, keep going until you document all important influences from your childhood and adolescence.

Completing this step will allow you an opportunity to see connections, themes, patterns or trends in your behaviors and choices. They will be in relation to experiences, people, situations, events, beliefs, internal conflicts, past trauma or losses from your childhood and adolescence. You will likely be surprised at what you uncover.

In order to proceed with this step, answer the following question:

What has contributed to you thinking/feeling this way in your childhood or adolescence?

Identify the times, specific to your childhood and adolescent years, where you have also experienced this thought or feeling so that you can uncover possible influences.

Keep reflecting and going deeper until all important factors have been written down.

Now it's time to write down factors that influenced your central thought in the childhood or adolescence.

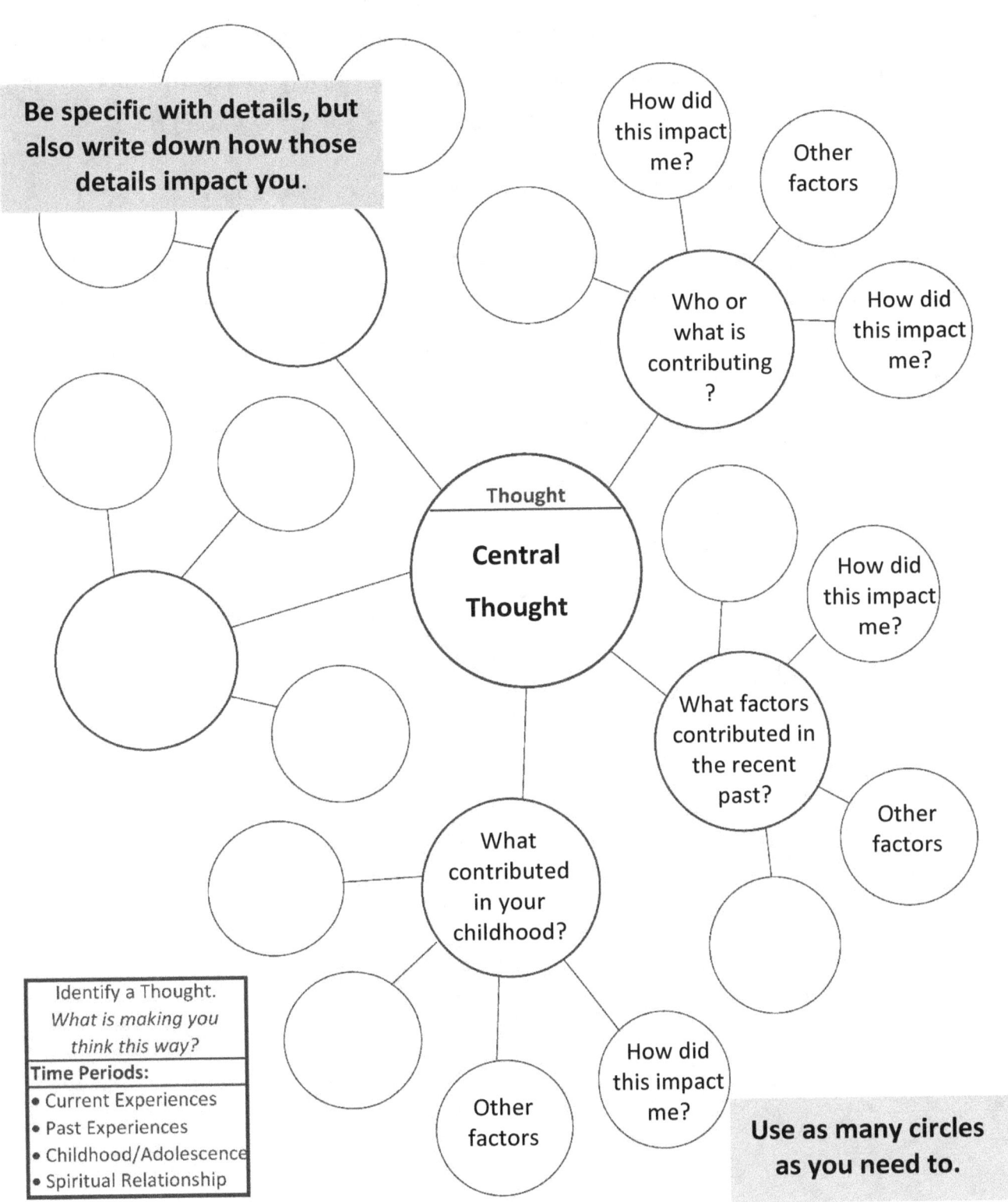

Be specific with details, but also write down how those details impact you.

How did this impact me?

Other factors

Who or what is contributing?

How did this impact me?

Thought

Central Thought

How did this impact me?

What factors contributed in the recent past?

Other factors

What contributed in your childhood?

How did this impact me?

Identify a Thought.
What is making you think this way?

Time Periods:
- Current Experiences
- Past Experiences
- Childhood/Adolescence
- Spiritual Relationship

Other factors

Use as many circles as you need to.

Spiritual Relationship

Next, in step five, you will analyze how your spirituality fits in and influences your central thought or feeling. This analysis could include factors related to your religious beliefs (or lack of), what you have been taught about spirituality, or your mindset about the world as a whole. In order to complete this step, answer the following question:

How is your central thought related to your spiritual relationships?

You will be taking an introspective dive here. Meditate on all of your feelings about your spiritual relationships. Be honest with yourself and allow yourself to be heard and understood. How do these feelings relate to your central thought or feeling and how have your spiritual experiences or thoughts contributed? Go a bit further and consider your spiritual relationships as a whole (related to your identified thought or feeling)?

Now it's time to write down factors that influenced your central thought in the in your spiritual relationship.

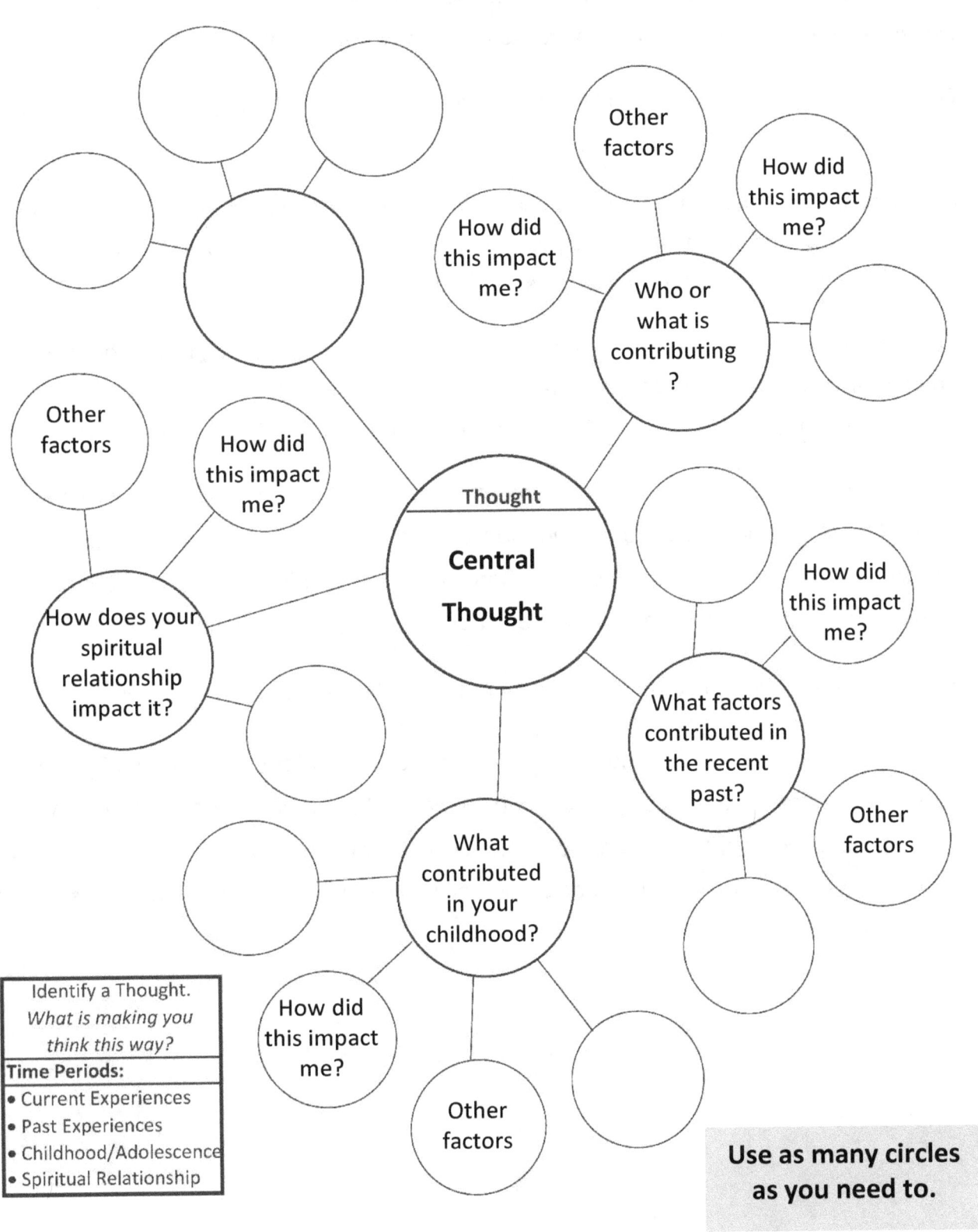

Identify a Thought.
What is making you think this way?

Time Periods:
- Current Experiences
- Past Experiences
- Childhood/Adolescence
- Spiritual Relationship

Use as many circles as you need to.

The Big Picture (Core Connections)

You made it to the final step in the Thought Mapping process (Element 1) which is to review all the factors that have been identified as related to your central thought.

Glance over what you have pinpointed so far. Is there anything else that you think should be added?

Do you see any themes or big picture connections? If you notice immediate links or themes, start to physically connect them on the paper. Use a colorful pen or marker and draw lines all over your map to link the repeating themes.

Spend some time focusing on these factors so that you can gain insight into how your present and past experiences are impacting the way you see the world, how they influence the way you behave, and how they affect the way you engage with others.

On the following pages, you will see some examples of my personal Thought Maps where I have included notes regarding the Core Connections that I have identified doing this type of review. We will go into Core Connections in greater detail in a later section of this workbook but reviewing them briefly now may help you in this section.

Now, it's time for you to complete your own review. When doing so:

- Look for themes involving your choices or behaviors (or in your thought patterns).
- Take note of contributing factors which may not have been dealt with or fully processed and, as such, are still impacting your current choices.
- Be gentle with yourself and give this activity the time needed to make those connections.

Have you completed your Thought Map? If yes, give yourself a pat on the back. Doing this process takes a lot of work and self-reflection so answer the following questions to check in with yourself about where you are.

How are you feeling about your experience while creating a Thought Map?

_____

_____

_____

_____

_____

_____

_____

You just went through a step-by-step process of learning how to complete a Thought Map.

The next couple of pages are Thought Maps I have completed in order to illustrate the process. Remember that I have been doing this on myself for over 10 years and I still come up with new insights. As an example, the Thought Map on "Tearful" was done recently because I was triggered and decided to put it to paper.

When reading my example Thought Maps, the top right circle includes current details, the bottom right involves the recent past, the very bottom is related to childhood, and the bottom left shows how my central thought relates to my Spiritual Relationship. I also identified and wrote down my Core Connections at the bottom of my maps.

Dr. B's Journey: ANGRY

We all get angry at times. It's only natural. Anger can often come up over simple things. If you look at my Thought Map, you'll notice that I'm actually angry at myself and at how hard things are for me. When I look at this map objectively, I notice (and have had to process) a perceived pattern of not living up to expectations. You may draw similar conclusions and begin to see your connections as well.

The Mentally STRONG Method: Element 1

Thought Map

Mentally STRONG

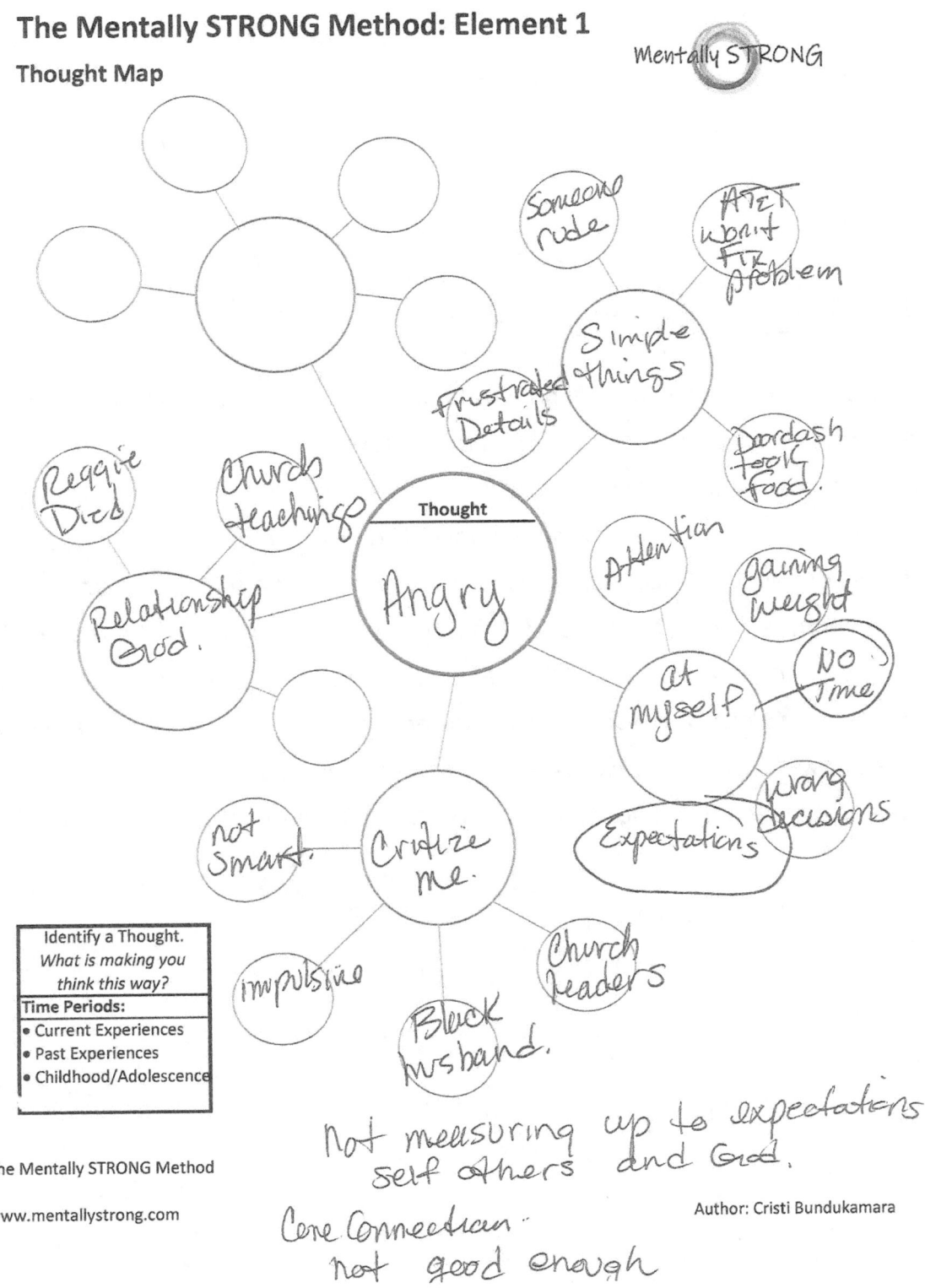

Someone rude

AT&T won't fix problem

Simple things

Frustrated Details

Dordash fook food.

Reggie Died

Church teachings

Thought

Angry

Attention

gaining weight

Relationship God.

at myself

NO Time

Expectations

wrong decisions

not Smart.

Critize me.

impulsive

Black husband.

Church leaders

Identify a Thought.
What is making you think this way?
Time Periods:
• Current Experiences
• Past Experiences
• Childhood/Adolescence

Not measuring up to expectations
self others and God.

Core Connection.
not good enough

The Mentally STRONG Method

www.mentallystrong.com

Author: Cristi Bundukamara

49

Dr. B's Journey: DEPRESSED

Here is another of my thought maps related to being depressed. I often find myself in a depressed mood when I feel overwhelmed with the expectations in my life. As I've mentioned, I have experienced a lot of grief (still do). The following map comes from mapping my symptoms for many years. The next two circles on the map are what I like to think of as "evidence that I am not good enough." I am aware after many years of working on myself that "I'm not good enough" is a Core Connection for me. Just knowing and understanding that fact makes this a useful map for me. When you acknowledge a Core Connection, it's encouraging because you can reframe it and let it go. I can now do so very quickly (with the practice I've had) and not allow it to significantly impact my thoughts and mood. You will get there, too.

The Mentally STRONG Method: Element 1

Thought Map

Mentally STRONG

Patients

Business

Tasks

Expectation

Family

Overwhelmed

hard not enough time

Thought

Depressed

Reggu

Johnny

No Rescue

not give what ask.

God Utopia not real for me.

trouble Feeling love.

wrong Grief.

Miah

Bundy

Family Close

Lack love.

Evidence not good enough

Fail

NOT like me

Critizized

| Identify a Thought. |
| *What is making you think this way?* |
| **Time Periods:** |
| • Current Experiences |
| • Past Experiences |
| • Childhood/Adolescence |

Core Connection : not good enough

The Mentally STRONG Method

www.mentallystrong.com

Author: Cristi Bundukamara

51

Dr. B's Journey: ANXIOUS

Anxiety? You're not alone. If you look through my anxious Thought Map, you will notice my grief and guilt around what I deem to be the "wrong decision" that I made on the day that my son Reggie died. You can listen to the whole story on my YouTube Channel (youtube.com/c/drbmentallystrong). This "decision" connects my thinking to the "bad decisions" of my past and also impacts my relationship with God (as identified on my Thought Map). I can further break it down in terms of how it influences me today and my persistent fear of making the wrong decisions.

I have learned, and you will learn too (in elements two and three) how to ORGANIZE and CHOOSE so that you will not allow these thoughts to negatively impact your current thoughts and mood.

The Mentally STRONG Method: Element 1

Thought Map

Mentally STRONG

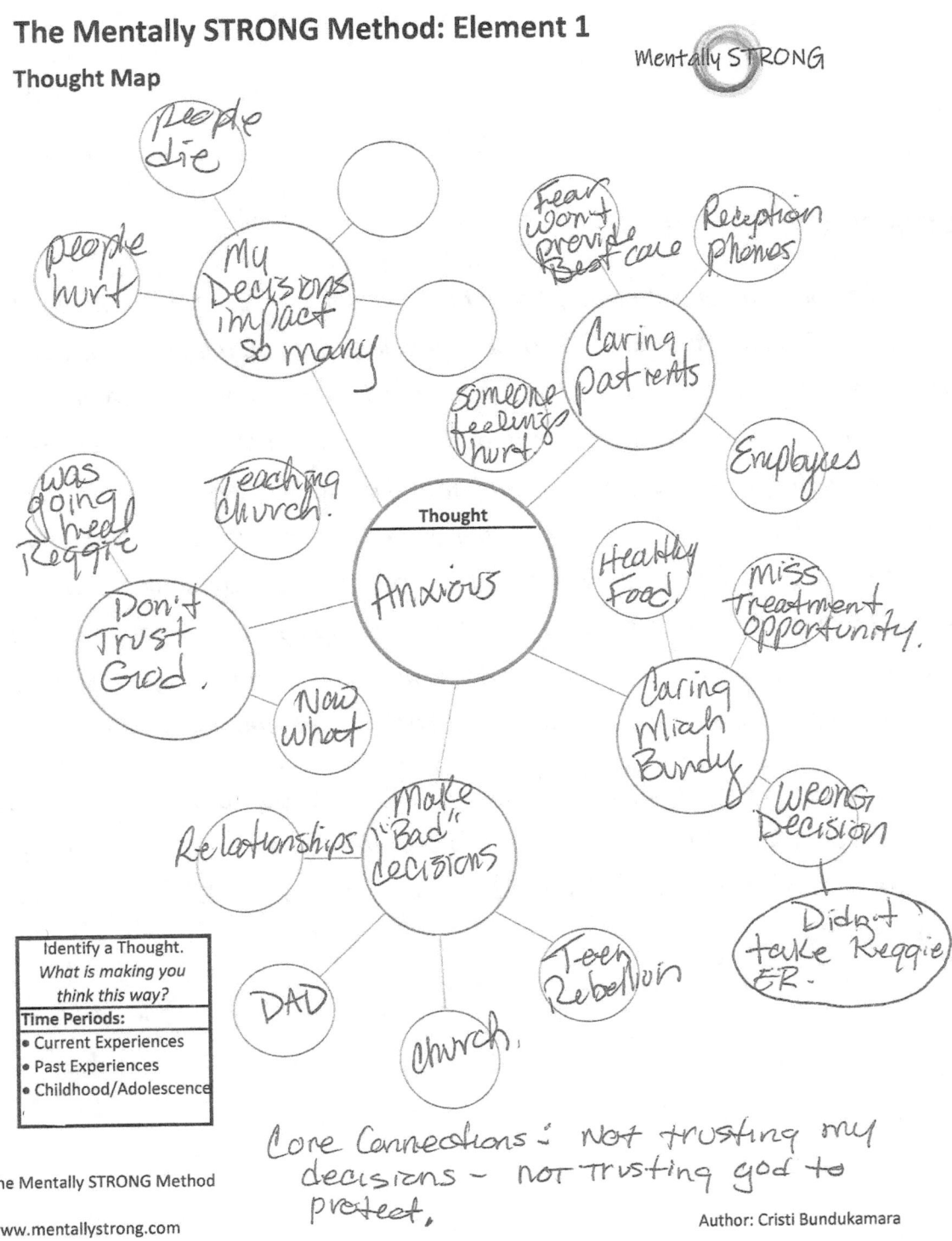

People die

People hurt

My Decisions impact so many

Fear won't provide Best care

Reception phones

Caring patients

Someone feelings hurt

Employees

was going heal Reggie

Teaching Church.

Thought

Anxious

Healthy Food

miss Treatment opportunity.

Don't Trust God.

Now what

Caring Miah Bundy

WRONG Decision

Didn't take Reggie ER.

Relationships

Make "Bad" decisions

DAD

Church,

Teen Rebellion

| Identify a Thought. |
| *What is making you think this way?* |
| **Time Periods:** |
| • Current Experiences |
| • Past Experiences |
| • Childhood/Adolescence |

Core Connections: Not trusting my decisions - not trusting god to protect,

The Mentally STRONG Method

www.mentallystrong.com

Author: Cristi Bundukamara

Thought Map: TEARFUL

The purpose of completing Thought Maps is to gain insight. If you look through my Tearful Thought Map, you will notice that in less than 10 minutes, I gained two new insights about myself. As you can imagine, after 10 years, I am very confident in the process and have gained significant understanding of myself and the way that I think. But I was getting triggered, so I dug deeper and found two new insights about myself. The first was that if I'm getting tearful when I don't feel sad, it can be because I am unable to communicate what I am thinking or feeling. In this particular situation, the feeling I couldn't communicate was that I happened to be wrong about a person. Coming to that realization was a big deal for me because I pride myself in my ability to understand people, so I was tearful when I didn't understand this person.

The other Thought Map examples were done retrospectively and simulate some of the Thought Maps that I have completed over the years. My goal is to give you ideas and examples of how Thought Maps can be profoundly insightful with just a short time commitment.

The Mentally STRONG Method: Element 1

Thought Map

Mentally STRONG

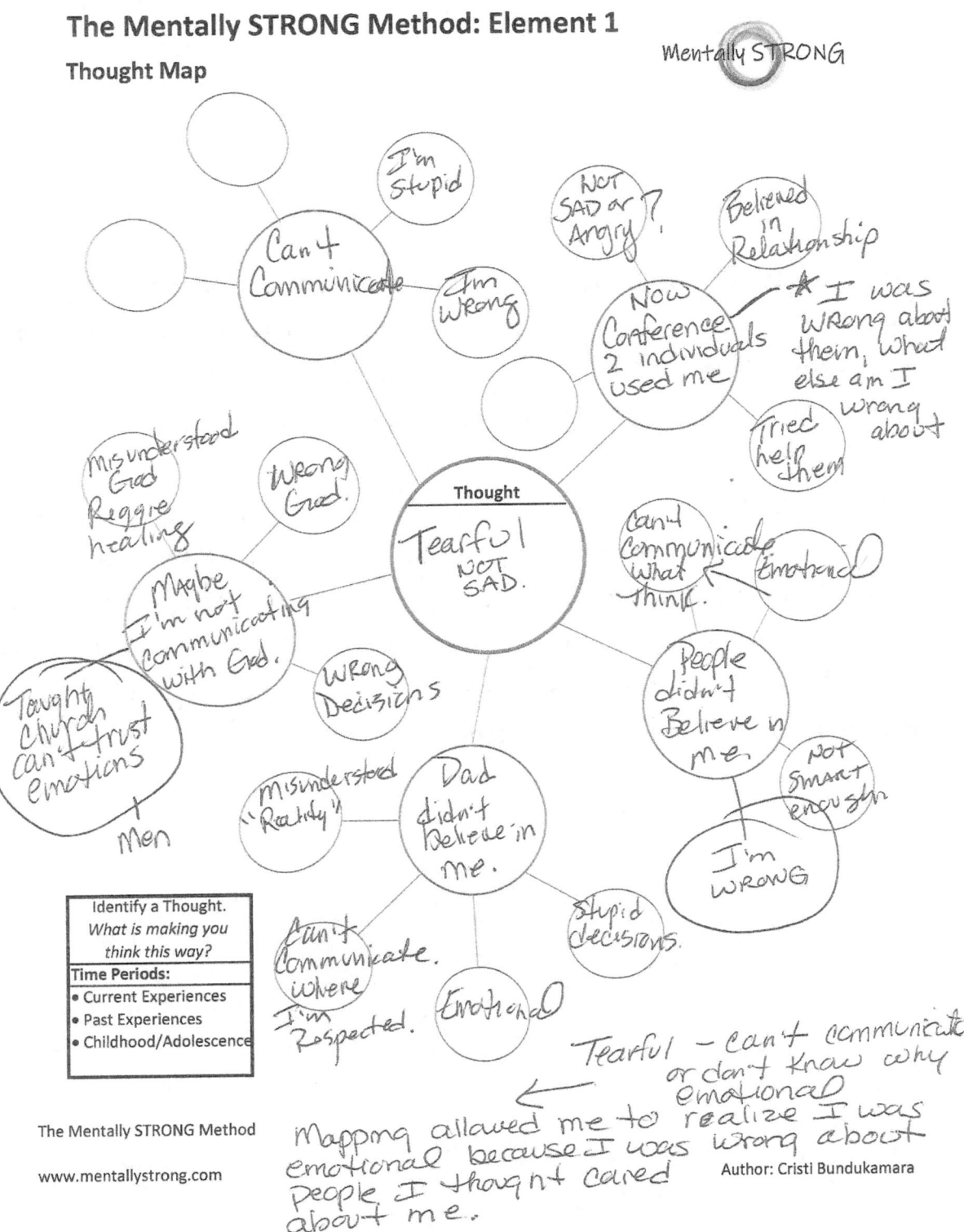

| Identify a Thought. |
| What is making you think this way? |

Time Periods:
- Current Experiences
- Past Experiences
- Childhood/Adolescence

The Mentally STRONG Method

www.mentallystrong.com

Author: Cristi Bundukamara

Tearful - can't communicate or don't know why emotional

Mapping allowed me to realize I was emotional because I was wrong about people I thought cared about me.

The process of Thought Mapping is a cathartic experience and should be done with the idea that you are going to release the identified emotions with the intent of moving forward to Elements 2-4. In those later Elements, you can ORGANIZE and CHOOSE actions and thoughts that are in line with your Personal Vision.

It is important not to spend too much time in the Thought Mapping process because it can lead to rumination rather than emotional release which is not what we want. Rumination is when you're thinking about something in particular and allowing its negative thoughts and emotions to fuel more negativity rather than pushing you to find strength or solutions. The goal of this process is not to ruminate, but to get to a place of strength and the ability to make positive choices.

Section 4

Element 2: Identify and Organize

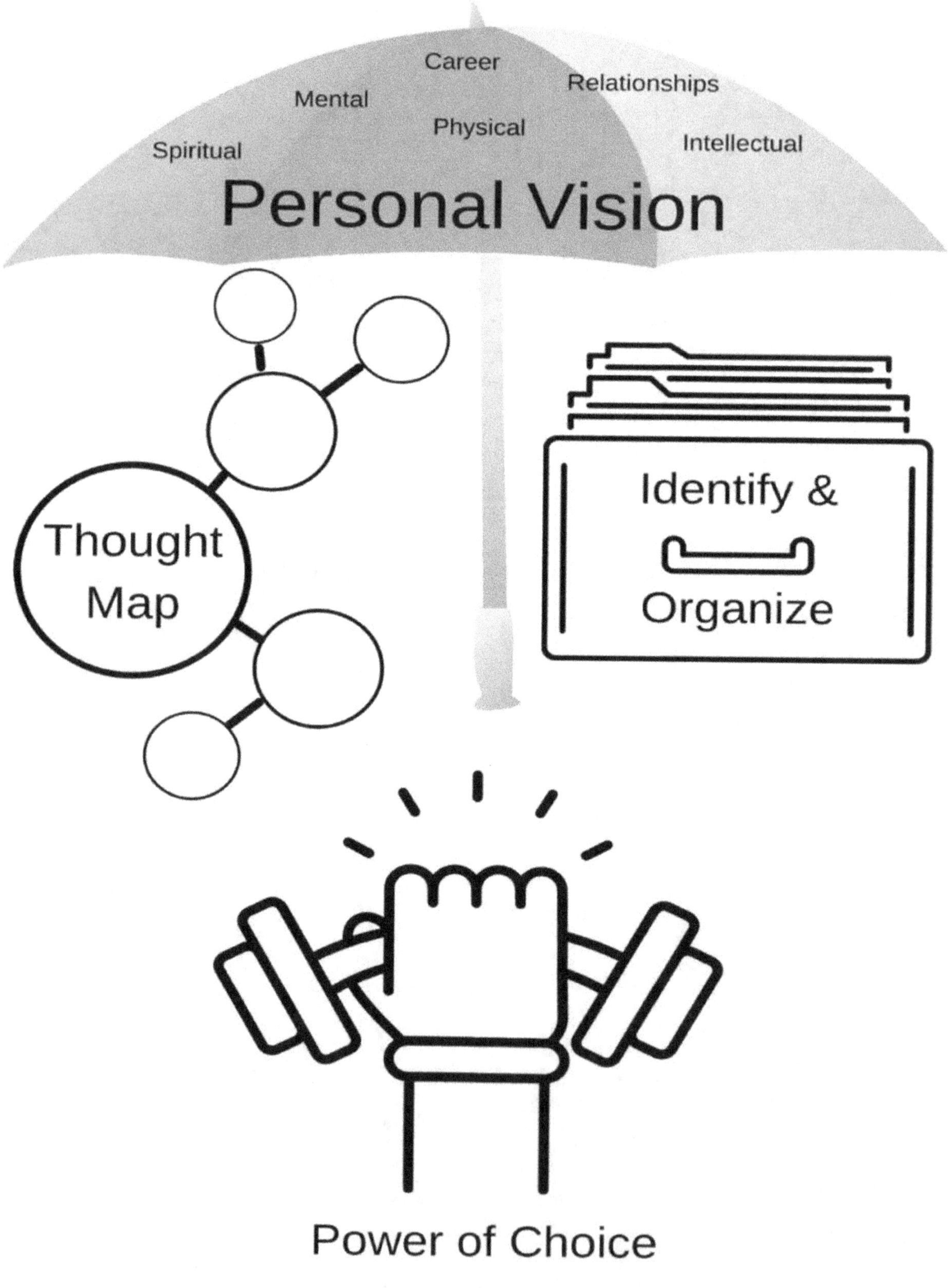

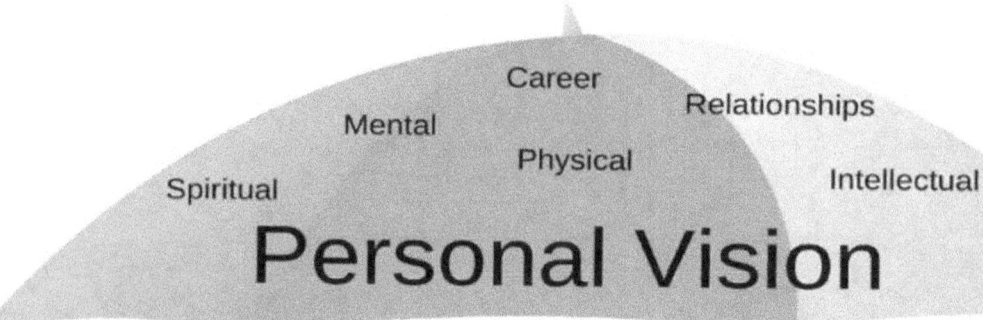

Career

Mental

Relationships

Spiritual

Physical

Intellectual

Personal Vision

Thought
Map

Identify &
Organize

Power of Choice

Element 2: Identify and Organize

Now that you've created your initial Thought Map, you are ready to move on to Element 2: Identify and Organize. This element of the Mentally STRONG Method is where you will identify and organize the contributing factors (all the "stuff") that you linked to your central thought in the Thought Map.

In this element is what I like to call placing influential factors into your METAPHORICAL FILE CABINET. Your file cabinet is a place to organize the mental pieces of your story (the ones that you identified while completing your Thought Map). Having this file cabinet in place will allow you to file all of the factors (that you previously identified) into 10 separate categories. With the organization of these factors, you will better be able to see how they are impacting your life today. Streamlining in this manner will also support you by empowering you to identify themes while discovering strategies that you can adapt moving forward.

When completing the Identify and Organize Element, here are some critical ideas to keep in mind:

- This element contains your metaphorical file cabinet for use in the identification and organization of your contributing factors.
- By organizing your thoughts or feelings into these categories, you can better process the factors into workable pieces.
- There can be some overlap with the same factor being filed in multiple categories.
- As you explore your identified factors and organize them into categories, remember that:
    - You do not have to put something in all ten categories.
    - Not every single item must be filled in or completed in each category.
    - There is no pressure to fill up the entire sheet.

As I mentioned, there are 10 categories, or drawers, within your metaphorical file cabinet. You'll notice that some of the factors may be filed in more than one category or not belong in any category at all at this time (and that's okay). When you are doing your filing, there are some critical points to consider as outlined on the following pages

But, before you get started with this second element, I want you to complete a Choice Opportunity Worksheet: The "Mentally STRONG Brain."

This "Mentally STRONG Brain" activity will deepen your understanding of how important it is to organize your brain. I placed this choice opportunity here to get you ready for filing the thoughts and feelings from your Thought Map. I often say that creating the Thought Map is like 20 years of journaling in 20 minutes. But, just like with journaling, if you don't move forward with ORGANIZING and CHOOSING, you will find yourself ruminating on your problems instead of finding your strength. And, hint, hint, I want you to find your strength.

Choice Opportunity: Mentally STRONG

Expected outcome: Visualize your default way of thinking and grow to have a more balanced way of thinking and organizing your brain.

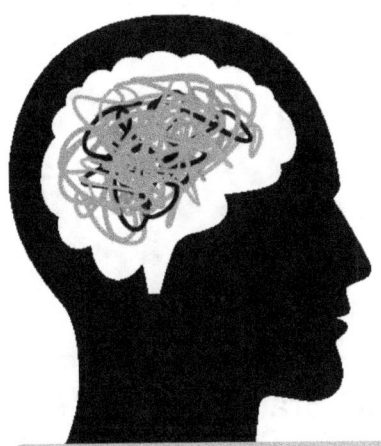 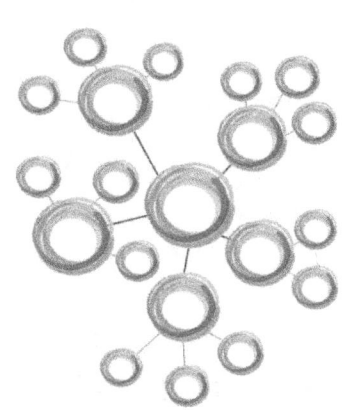 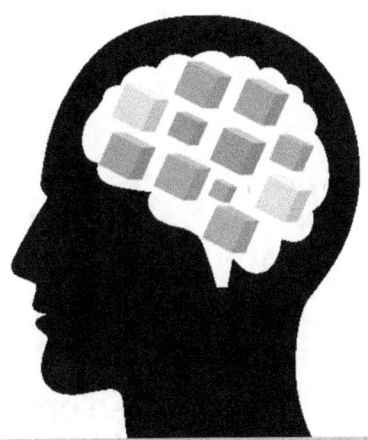

Disorganized Brain	Mentally STRONG Brain	Compartmentalized Brain
• Everything is connected • Emotionally Charged	• Find Insight into connections • Organize • Choose	• Everything in boxes • Nothing is connected • Deal with one box at a time

Where are you on this continuum?

Be honest with yourself and circle a number

0   1   2   3   4   5   6   7   8   9   10

If you are closer to 0 or 1 than you are to 5, we encourage you to move ➡ on the continuum and If you are closer to 9 or 10 on the continuum, we encourage you to move ⬅ on the continuum with the goal being as close to the middle as possible.

Challenge Yourself: Now that you have insight into where you are on the continuum, brainstorm some ways and some choice you can make to get closer to the middle and a more balanced way of thinking:

_____

_____

_____

This is your *Choice Opportunity* to develop a Mentally STRONG® brain.

Learn more about *The Mentally STRONG Method*: 1-800-55-STRONG ~ www.mentallystrong.com

"An organized Brain is a Mentally STRONG Brain"

-   *Dr. B*

Using the next worksheet, you will document Elements 2 and 3. Feel free to tear out the page or copy it to follow along. Because it is a file cabinet, you can keep adding to it with each Thought Map you complete. Your file cabinet will grow over time.

(Tear me out or copy)

Identify & Organize	Power of Choice
Core Connections	
Triggers	
Grief	
Trauma	
Negative Thoughts　　Rating　(Belief) _____/10 _____/10 _____/10	
Behaviors/Choices	
Anxiety/Worry　　Rating (Time Spent) _____/10 _____/10 _____/10	
Injustices	
Spiritual Conflict	
Addiction	

(Tear me out or copy)

Identify & Organize	Power of Choice
Core Connections	
Triggers	
Grief	
Trauma	
Negative Thoughts Rating (Belief) _____/10 _____/10 _____/10	
Behaviors/Choices	
Anxiety/Worry Rating (Time Spent) _____/10 _____/10 _____/10	
Injustices	
Spiritual Conflict	
Addiction	

The Ten Categories

Next, I will walk you through each of the 10 categories. The identification and organization of your contributing factors from the Thought Map will be based on what is really impacting the identified central thought or feeling listed in the middle circle of your Thought Map. Each of these categories is important and distinct and any of the factors you have written on your Thought Map will be able to fit into one of these categories.

Follow along with me through each of the categories below and organize your own factors into the Ten Categories. The following are the ten categories of the Mentally STRONG Method:

- Core Connections
- Trigger
- Grief
- Trauma
- Negative Thought

- Behaviors/Choices
- Anxiety/Worry
- Injustice
- Spiritual Conflict
- Addiction

After each explanation of a category, I will give personal examples from that category and also there will be one or more Choice Opportunities related to the category.

Trigger

The first category in your file cabinet is Core Connections; however, we are going to skip that one for now and work on it later. (Don't worry, we will come back to Core Connections at the very end. Just leave it blank for now).

Let's look at the next category in your file cabinet: Triggers. A trigger is an external stimulus that pushes a "button" and causes a response or reaction within you. A trigger is usually not positive and can indicate a limit, boundary, or reactive behavior. It can also be indicative of an intolerance to certain behaviors or things that bother you. You may not always be aware of a trigger or how it impacts you or your choices and behaviors. It is important, however, to be able to recognize and identify your trigger(s) so that you can process them and recognize their influence moving forward. Although triggers are external in nature, they cause a reaction within you.

As part of this process, it's vital to understand that you don't have control of when and where you'll encounter triggers. What you do have control over is your response and reaction to the trigger. The more that you are able to realize that the trigger is not the *real problem*, the less it will control you with a negative response or reaction. Controlling your response to the trigger and/or choosing to respond differently is what gives you mental strength. And, as you know, your goal is to become Mentally STRONG. As such, let's do the work to pinpoint those triggers (and file them) using the instructions below.

Identifying your Trigger(s) from the Thought Map

- Identify items within your Thought Map that trigger you to have a reaction.
- If you do not identify any triggers in your Thought Map, then move on to the next category.
- Examples of possible triggers:
    - Disrespect
    - Bringing attention to a flaw
    - Expectation
    - Judgement
    - Loss of control

Now it's time to complete this category (Trigger) for yourself:

Identify & Organize	Power of Choice
Core Connections Leave this blank for now, we will come back to it.	
Triggers • List the triggers in your Thought Map, these are external factors that are causing a reaction.	
Grief	
Trauma	
Negative Thoughts Rating (Belief) _____/10 _____/10 _____/10	
Behaviors/Choices	
Anxiety/Worry Rating (Time Spent) _____/10 _____/10 _____/10	
Injustices	
Spiritual Conflict	
Addiction	

Grief

The next category in your file cabinet is grief. Grief is complex. Grief is a loss. The loss can be related to many things, including the loss of a loved one, a relationship, a dream, or an expectation. Grief typically involves much more than just losing a person and can often be difficult to recognize. You may not identify the loss of something as grief, but any significant loss is something that needs to be grieved. Again, this could be the loss of a dream, an opportunity, the loss of potential, the loss of an experience, and more. Grief can be so many things which is why it's important to address.

To put more context around this, here's an example: *I have a child that can no longer walk, run, or participate in track. I need to alter the dream I had of my child becoming a track star. That original dream is lost, and unachievable as once dreamed. As such, I need to grieve the loss of this dream. After properly grieving, I can now create a new dream by choosing to adapt to that loss.*

Identifying Grief from the Thought Map

So, let's begin this process of pinpointing your grief (and filing it) as outlined below:

- Identify your grief within your Thought Map.
- What have you lost? When were you disappointed over something that did not turn out the way you wanted it to? Your losses should be grieved.
- Acknowledging grief may be a life-long process that comes with feeling the associated pain (and that's critical for processing).

Examples of grief- related events that are non-death losses include:

- The end of a relationship
- Dysfunctional relationships
- Losing your home or changes in living situations
- Loss of business, a job, or retiring
- Medical diagnoses (grieve if this applies to you or a loved one)
- Anticipatory grief (hospice, terminal illness, or chronic disease)

Now it's time to complete this category (Grief) for yourself:

Identify & Organize	Power of Choice
Core Connections Leave this blank for now, we will come back to it.	
Triggers • List the triggers in your Thought Map, these are external factors that are causing a reaction.	
Grief • List the loss in your Thought Map here	
Trauma	
Negative Thoughts Rating (Belief) _____/10 _____/10 _____/10	
Behaviors/Choices	
Anxiety/Worry Rating (Time Spent) _____/10 _____/10 _____/10	
Injustices	
Spiritual Conflict	
Addiction	

Trauma

The fourth category in your file cabinet is trauma. Trauma is defined as a distressing or disturbing experience. Your trauma can be physical, mental, emotional, sexual, or psychological. The experience of trauma usually results from an overwhelming amount of stress that exceeds our ability to cope. It also includes how we integrate our thoughts related to that experience.

Survivors of abuse, violent crimes, and other life-changing events need to process the trauma they've experienced. It is crucial to manage the trauma you've undergone in your life in order to minimize its impact on your choices and behaviors (both now and in the future).

So, let's begin this process of pinpointing your trauma (and filing it) as outlined below:

Identifying Trauma from the Thought Map

- Examples of trauma include:
    - Sexual abuse
    - Verbal abuse
    - Physical abuse
    - Mental/Emotional abuse
    - Witness to abuse, a violent crime, drug use
    - Victim/survivor of a crime
    - Domestic violence
    - Parental drug use resulting in neglect

Reminder: You do not need to use every category or item. If you have not experienced Trauma, you can leave this part blank. This is a protective factor that you can be grateful for.

Consider this key point regarding Trauma: The purpose of identifying trauma is NOT to dig up, re-live memories, or to reopen old wounds. The goal is to recognize patterns and connections that impact who you are today, and how you react.

Now it's time to complete this category (Trauma) for yourself:

Identify & Organize	Power of Choice
Core Connections Leave this blank for now, we will come back to it.	
Triggers • List the triggers in your Thought Map, these are external factors that are causing a reaction.	
Grief • List the loss in your Thought Map here	
Trauma • List any trauma from your Thought Map here, you can leave items blank if needed	
Negative Thoughts Rating (Belief) _____ /10 _____ /10 _____ /10	
Behaviors/Choices	
Anxiety/Worry Rating (Time Spent) _____ /10 _____ /10 _____ /10	
Injustices	
Spiritual Conflict	
Addiction	

<u>Negative Thought</u>

The fifth category in your file cabinet is negative thought(s). A negative thought is an internal narrative that occurs while you are contemplating something. Most likely, you do not even realize that you are thinking a negative thought until someone else brings it to your attention; these negative thoughts are automatic and ingrained in you due to life-long patterns. As such, it is important that these negative thoughts be identified, and that steps are taken so that you can stop them from taking over. This is a big internal change and will take practice and time. But with a conscious effort, you can modify your thinking and decrease the presence of the negative thought(s). *So, let's begin this process of pinpointing our negative thought(s) (and filing them) as outlined below:*

Identify Negative Thoughts and Then Rate Them:

1. Identify and list the negative thought(s) that were identified in your Thought Map.
2. Consider why you believe the negative thought(s). Are they true? Are they thoughts that you claim for yourself based on what others have told you at some point in your life?
3. Rate your negative thoughts on a scale from 0-10. This rating is based on how much you really believe this thought today. A 0 means that you don't believe the thought at all, and a 10 means that you completely believe it (100%).

Consider some key points regarding Negative Thoughts while completing this activity:

- They are negative things you say to yourself about yourself.
- Negative thoughts are self-defeating choices that undermine your opportunity to be successful and content with yourself.
- It is important that you are honest with yourself in identifying the thoughts occurring in your head that are not positive.
- The first step in loving yourself is speaking kindly to yourself.

Now it's time for you to complete this category (Negative Thoughts) for yourself:

Identify & Organize	Power of Choice
Core Connection Leave this blank for now, we will come back to it.	
Triggers • List the triggers in your Thought Map, these are external factors that are causing a reaction.	
Grief • List the loss in your Thought Map here	
Trauma • List any trauma from your Thought Map here, you can leave items blank if needed	
Negative Thoughts　　　　Rating　(Belief) • List the negative thoughts here _____ /10 　and rate how much you believe _____ /10 　them.　_____ /10	
Behaviors/Choices	
Anxiety/Worry　　　　Rating (Time Spent) _____ /10 _____ /10 _____ /10	
Injustices	
Spiritual Conflict	
Addiction	

Behaviors & Choices

The sixth category in your file cabinet is Behaviors & Choices. Behaviors and choices can be counterproductive and maladaptive and can include coping strategies that you are not aware of. These behaviors are often protective in nature but are no longer serving your best interest, so it's critical to identify those that are not supportive of your Personal Vision, and that may be contributing to the central thought or feeling that you identified (in the Thought Map).

Identifying Behaviors & Choices from the Thought Map

So, let's begin this process of pinpointing our behavior/choices (and filing them) as outlined below:

1. Identify your behaviors- those that are not serving you well.
2. Include self-destructive behaviors, unproductive behaviors, inappropriate behaviors, avoidance behaviors, and dysfunctional coping mechanisms.
3. Identify behaviors that are contrary to what you want.
4. Identify behaviors that are not in line with your personal belief system.
5. Identify past/present choices that are contributing.
6. Identify consequences that you are ignoring.

Consider this key point regarding Behaviors & Choices while completing this activity:

- Focusing on acknowledging your behaviors/choices is designed to promote change, not to evoke negative thoughts about your behaviors.

Now it's time for you to complete this category (Behaviors & Choices) for yourself.

Identify & Organize	Power of Choice
Core Connections Leave this blank for now, we will come back to it.	
Triggers • List the triggers in your Thought Map, these are external factors that are causing a reaction.	
Grief • List the loss in your Thought Map here	
Trauma • List any trauma from your Thought Map here, you can leave items blank if needed	
Negative Thoughts　　　　　**Rating　(Belief)** • List the negative thought here and rate _____ /10 　 how much you believe them.　　　　　_____ /10 　　　　　　　　　　　　　　　　　　　　 _____ /10	
Behaviors/Choices • Do you have any behaviors or choices in your Thought Map?	
Anxiety/Worry　　　　**Rating (Time Spent)** 　　　　　　　　　　　　　　_____ /10 　　　　　　　　　　　　　　_____ /10 　　　　　　　　　　　　　　_____ /10	
Injustices	
Spiritual Conflict	
Addiction	

Anxiety & Worry

The seventh category in your file cabinet is Anxiety & Worry. Anxiety can be a normal, healthy feeling, but when anxiety is consuming your every thought and impacting your actions, then it is essential to recognize the disproportionate amount of stress you are experiencing. In this case, anxiety becomes overwhelming and leads to worry and fear. At this point, it is considered maladaptive and can interfere with your life.

Stress is a form of anxiety that, when prolonged and out of proportion to the situation, can lead to increased nervousness, impaired coping abilities, and ineffective decision making. Excessive anxiety is characterized by extreme nervousness, fear, apprehension, or worry leading you to be ineffective in your own life.

Identifying Anxiety & Worry from the Thought Map

So, let's begin the process of pinpointing our anxiety/worry (and filing it) as outlined below:

1. Identify and list the anxiety and worry that you outlined in your Thought Map.
2. Rate the anxiety or worry from 0-10 based on how much time you spend consumed by it in a day. A score of 0 means that you spend little to no time worrying and a score of 10 means that you worry excessively about it or spend 100% of your time worrying about it.

Reminder: You do not need to use every category or item.

Consider this key point regarding Anxiety & Worry while working on this activity:

- If you have learned only one thing about anxiety and worry, it should be that you DO have control of your thoughts and anxiety.

Now it's time for you to complete this category (Anxiety & Worry) for yourself.

Identify & Organize	Power of Choice
Core Connections Leave this blank for now, we will come back to it.	
Triggers • List the triggers in your Thought Map, these are external factors that are causing a reaction.	
Grief • List the loss in your Thought Map here	
Trauma • List any trauma from your Thought Map here, you can leave items blank if needed	
Negative Thoughts **Rating (Belief)** • List the negative thought here and rate _____/10 how much you believe them. _____/10 _____/10	
Behaviors/Choices • Do you have any behaviors or choices in your Thought Map?	
Anxiety/Worry **Rating (Time Spent)** • What worries came up, and rate _____/10 how much time do you spend? _____/10 _____/10	
Injustices	
Spiritual Conflict	
Addiction	

Injustice

The eighth category in your file cabinet is injustice. Injustices are unfair inequalities or treatments based on cultural, social, or political influences. Injustices can include racism, gender roles, societal expectations, divorce, custody battles, and more. The expectations imposed upon you from family, friends, or your employer are also examples. There are many injustices in this world that impact how others treat you.

Identifying Injustice from the Thought Map

So, let's begin this process of pinpointing our experiences with injustice (and file them) as outlined below:

Identify the injustices that came up in your Thought Map. They can include:

- Pre-Judgement
- Prejudice
- Racism
- Inequality
- Gender Roles
- Social Expectations
- Unfair Treatment
- Karma/Bad things happening to good people

Consider these key points regarding Injustice when completing this activity:

- You may not be able to change the injustices of the world, but you can change how you respond.
- When completing this element, avoid blanket statements like "All _____ are _____."

Now it's time for you to complete this category (Injustice) for yourself.

Identify & Organize	Power of Choice
Core Connections Leave this blank for now, we will come back to it.	
Triggers • List the triggers in your Thought Map, these are external factors that are causing a reaction.	
Grief • List the loss in your Thought Map here	
Trauma • List any trauma from your Thought Map here, you can leave items blank if needed	
Negative Thoughts **Rating (Belief)** • List the negative thought here and rate _____/10 how much you believe them. _____/10 _____/10	
Behaviors/Choices • Do you have any behaviors or choices in your Thought Map?	
Anxiety/Worry **Rating (Time Spent)** • What worries came up, and rate _____/10 how much time do you spend? _____/10 _____/10	
Injustices • Write down any injustice that came up in your Thought Map	
Spiritual Conflict	
Addiction	

Spiritual Conflict

The ninth category in your file cabinet is spiritual conflict. *Spiritual Conflict occurs when your belief does not match your experience.* You might blame a deity (like God) or the universe for something that has happened to you. Or you might think that the deity (or the universe) is responsible for something specific happening in your life. As such, you may not have a good spiritual relationship, or you may question your devotion to that deity (i.e., God) or the universe. Getting to the bottom of this spiritual influence is imperative for your forward momentum.

Identifying Spiritual Conflict from the Thought Map

So, let's begin the process of pinpointing your experience with spiritual conflict (and filing it) as outlined below:

1. Identify the factors in your relationship with **a deity or the universe.**
2. Identify your thoughts or feelings about this deity or the universe that may be contributing to your identified thoughts from your Thought Map.
3. Identify areas where you question if this deity or the universe is contributing to the identified thought or feeling from your Thought Map.

Reminder: You do not need to fill in every line of the category.

Examples include:

- You want to or have been taught to believe in God, but when you pray you feel or experience nothing.
- In my life, my biggest spiritual conflict is that I believed that God would heal my son and my son died.
- Also, I believed that if I followed God's "rules", good things would happen, but if I continued to experience unimaginable hardship.

<u>Now it's time for you to complete this category (Spiritual Conflict) for yourself.</u>

Identify & Organize	Power of Choice
Core Connections Leave this blank for now, we will come back to it.	
Triggers • List the triggers in your Thought Map, these are external factors that are causing a reaction.	
Grief • List the loss in your Thought Map here	
Trauma • List any trauma from your Thought Map here, you can leave items blank if needed	

Negative Thoughts   Rating   (Belief)
• List the negative thought here and rate _____/10
  how much you believe them. _____/10
  _____/10	

Behaviors/Choices • Do you have any behaviors or choices in your Thought Map?	

Anxiety/Worry   Rating (Time Spent)
• What worries came up, and rate _____/10
  how much time do you spend? _____/10
  _____/10	

Injustices • Write down any injustice that came up in your Thought Map	
Spiritual Conflict • Write down any spiritual conflict that came up in your Thought Map	
Addiction	

Author: Cristi Bundukamara

Addiction

The tenth and final category in your file cabinet is addiction. Addiction is a disorder in thinking that is observed to be a compulsive need to engage in rewarding stimuli, despite the negative consequences to the choice of those behaviors. Addiction is very complex and involves the chemical neurofeedback within the brain of the person who is addicted. An addiction can be to alcohol, drugs, gambling, shopping, sex, food, or other behaviors/actions that can negatively impact your life.

It's key to note your addiction has a powerful impact on the lives of others as well (not just you or the person suffering from the addiction).

Identifying Addiction from the Thought Map
So, let's begin this process of pinpointing your experience with addiction (and filing it) as outlined below:

1. Identify things that you are or have been addicted to.
2. Identify the impact your addiction has had on others.

Reminder: You do not need to fill in every line of the category.

Consider this key point regarding Addiction:

- You should address addiction in multiple areas at the same time: environment, learned behaviors, untreated mental health, reward systems, and personal choices.

<u>Now it's time for you to complete this category (Addiction) for yourself.</u>

Identify & Organize	Power of Choice
Core Connections Leave this blank for now, we will come back to it.	
Triggers • List the triggers in your Thought Map, these are external factors that are causing a reaction.	
Grief • List the loss in your Thought Map here	
Trauma • List any trauma from your Thought Map here, you can leave items blank if needed	
Negative Thoughts **Rating (Belief)** • List the negative thought here and rate _____ /10 how much you believe them. _____ /10 _____ /10	
Behaviors/Choices • Do you have any behaviors or choices in your Thought Map?	
Anxiety/Worry **Rating (Time Spent)** • What worries came up for you? _____ /10 Rate how much time you spent. _____ /10 _____ /10	
Injustices • Write down any injustice that came up in your Thought Map	
Spiritual Conflict • Write down any spiritual conflict that came up in your Thought Map	
Addiction • Write down any addiction that may have come up in your Thought Map.	

Congratulations. You've completed the second element of this process. Keep this initial sheet to Identify and Organize for future Thought Maps. This is a compounding element, just like a file cabinet in your brain. The purpose is to help you organize factors into manageable pieces.

You are putting in the time to hone and develop your mental strength. Go you! Answer the following questions to reflect upon where you are at in the process.

How are you feeling about your experience with the Identify and Organize Elements?

_____

_____

_____

_____

_____

_____

_____

_____

_____

_____

_____

Why do we need to organize our thoughts, feelings, and problems into categories? The ORGANIZE in the THINK, ORGANIZE, and CHOOSE is not typical with other cognitive behavioral techniques. I created this element (ORGANIZE) as I worked through cognitive behavioral techniques on myself and began to realize that the process needed more and that there is not one technique that works for everything.

For example, the most popular and well-studied technique is to reframe negative thought processes into positive self-talk. This is a very effective technique for my negative self-talk, but it did not help with my grief, trauma, or addictive tendencies. Even more importantly, trying to reframe and think positively caused a spiritual conflict for me (when my positive thoughts/prayers were not confirmed by the tragic realities happening to me).

You have reviewed some of my Thought Maps, and, on the next page, you can see what categories I placed my thoughts, feelings, and problems into.

Identify & Organize	Power of Choice
The Mentally STRONG Method: Element 2	The Mentally STRONG Method: Element 3

Core Connections
- NOT Good enough
-

Triggers
- Wrong decision
- insinuate I'm not smart.
- Weight gain

Grief
- Reggie 17yo son died. DRPLA.
- Johnny 13yo died drowning
- Antisipatory grief Miah.

Trauma
- Date Rape
- Physical/Emotional Abuse
-

Negative Thoughts   Rating (Belief)
- Not smart   3 /10
- Fat   4 /10
-           /10

Behaviors/Choices
- impulsive
-
-

Anxiety/Worry   Rating (Time Spent)
- Wrong decisions.   4 /10
-            /10
-            /10

Injustices
- NOT Fair amount hardship
- NOT Fair ultra rare no treatment
- African Spouce + children

Spiritual Conflict
- Trusting God's Voice
-          Protection
-             love

Addiction
- Fear getting addicted.
-

<u>Activity Time!</u>

In preparation for the next chapter, I want you to work through the Choice Opportunity on the following page: Think, Organize and Choose. The whole Mentally STRONG Method can be simplified into those three words (Think, Organize, Choose). The "Think, Organize and Choose" Choice Opportunity is useful for understanding the whole process or can be used to quickly work through thoughts and feelings in a practical on-the-move kind of way.

Choice Opportunity: Think, Organize, Choose

Expected outcome: To learn the fundamentals of the Mentally STRONG Method in order to gain control of your thoughts, organize them, and create a plan to move ahead with confidence.

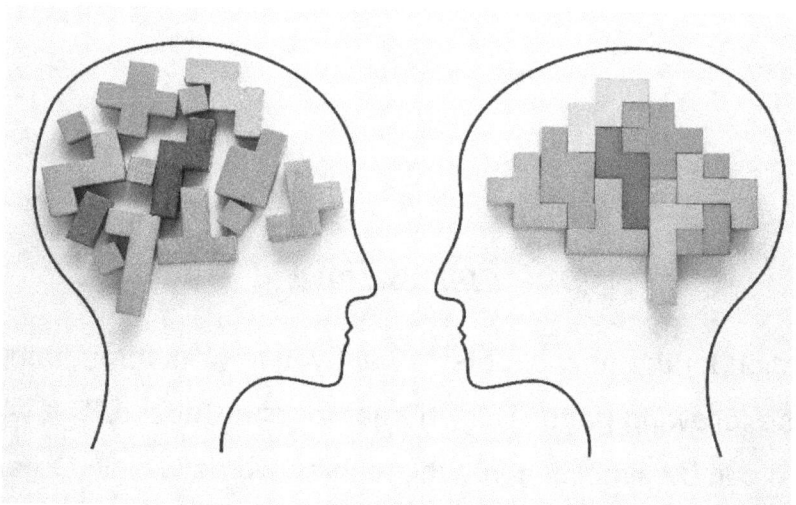

Step 1: What do you think the problem is?

_____

_____

Step 2: Take a deep breath/use grounding techniques to gain control of your thoughts.

The grounding technique you chose to use:

_____

_____

Step 3: Check the below categories to which these thoughts apply.

☐ Core Connections   ☐ Trauma
    ☐ Trigger   ☐ Negative Thought
    ☐ Grief   ☐ Behaviors/Choices

Learn more about *The Mentally STRONG Method*: **1-800-55-STRONG ~ www.mentallystrong.com**

☐ Anxiety/Worry   ☐ Spiritual Conflict
☐ Injustice   ☐ Addiction

Step 4: What positive choices are you going to make regarding each checked box?

_____

_____

_____

Step 5: Is this an organized plan that you can execute?

☐ Yes   ☐ No

If not, go back to through this quick process or go through complete process of The Mentally STRONG Method.

This is the basis of the mentally strong method. If you found this process difficult and were unable to organize your thoughts or create a plan with confidence, we encourage you to utilize the abundance of resources within the MSM.

This is your Choice Opportunity to be Mentally STRONG™. Think, organize, and choose!

It's just about time to move on to the next section of the method which is by far the most important (The Power of Choice). As a warning, it's also going to be a difficult section and will involve a lifetime process in which you are continuing to choose thoughts, feelings, and behaviors that are in line with your Personal Vision. In making these choices, you will not allow your current situation or past experiences to hold you back (you've got this!).

Each of the Choice Opportunities that you'll encounter are related to categories that are designed to help you with your Mental Health journey. We currently have over 100 Choice Opportunities and are continuing to develop new worksheets every day. Each category will introduce you to at least one Choice Opportunity that will help you process items in that category. Remember there is always more that you can do in the process of choosing.

Section 5

The Power of Choice

Power of Choice

Element 3: Power of Choice

We've reached the third element in the Mentally STRONG Method, the Power of Choice. The Power of Choice area deals with how you choose to respond to each of the items that you have identified and organized in the previous two elements. This third element is the spot where you have the power to decide about the items that you've already listed in each of the categories in your file cabinet. Using the file cabinet, you will be able to better see the value, importance, and priority of these items.

Here, in this element, you can choose to understand and process the smaller, workable pieces of your Thought Map. This third element involves utilizing the Mentally Strong Method Choice Opportunity worksheets in order to gain both understanding and the ability to change.

Choice Opportunities: Choice Opportunities are specifically designed worksheets created to challenge individuals to analyze their identified areas to gain insight into their thoughts/behaviors and to promote change. Completing these worksheets can help guide you through areas that you want to improve.

In this third element (Power of Choice), you will have endless opportunities to understand yourself, make choices, and discover your mental strength. Utilizing the Power of Choice is a process as well as a lifelong journey. Do not expect to make all of these choices in one session. You will continue to make new choices over time. As you do the work, making choices in this element and taking steps towards fulfilling them, it will bring you closer to your Personal Vision and the hopes, dreams, desires, and goals that you have set for yourself.

When working in this third element, the Power of Choice, here are some important points to consider:

- The second element (Identify & Organize) and the third element (Power of Choice) are closely connected and can be worked on at the same time in many instances. Be flexible and willing to move in and out of these elements simultaneously.

- On the worksheet, in the column to the right, you will write what you choose to do with the items you've listed in the categories.

- Working on personal growth takes times. It is not a race to be completed in one day. You **should not** expect yourself to recognize, fix, and change everything today.

- You will continue to have thought patterns and behaviors to work on.

- You can do this, but you must choose to do it. It may be one of the hardest things for you to tackle, but it will also be the most rewarding and life changing.

- Take the time to think and make conscious choices to bring about positive outcomes.

- Keep the categories organized and do not allow them to spill over into the other categories.

So, let's begin working on this third element by taking the initial step. You will first look at your trigger(s). Throughout this section, I will give a personal example of my "Power of Choice" in each category. Then, at the end, you will see my personal worksheet with these choices listed as a reminder to myself.

Trigger

Start with the second box on your worksheet: the one labeled "Trigger." (Again, we will talk about the Core Connections box at the end of this element so you can skip over it for now). In this category, you will do/consider the following:

- Meditate on the items that you listed as a trigger.
- Identify the underlying thought or feeling that is being triggered and why. You will likely have to dig deeper into your reaction for more clarity.
- The triggers usually stem from a negative belief or experience.
- Your goal is to prepare yourself to release the trigger and choose to have a decreased reaction each time.
- If the concept of letting go or releasing causes an emotional response, then you should do another Thought Map on the thought or feeling evoked before proceeding here.

Dr. B's Journey

We all have triggers. There is so much power in just recognizing what they are. Here are some of mine:

- I am personally triggered when something in my environment supports my negative beliefs or Core Connections.

- I am personally triggered when someone corrects me and I feel like I am not smart (negative thought).

- I am personally triggered when I do something wrong. Again, it makes me feel like I am not smart.

- I am personally triggered when something is difficult for me, even something small like trying to change my password and the software won't accept multiple attempts. It makes me feel like everything is hard for me (Core Connection).

My triggers will always be there (yours will too), but we have the power to choose whether or not to react to them. I have been practicing not reacting to my triggers for a long time. I can now almost immediately let them go. Sometimes, however, when multiple triggers are happening all at once, it brings me to a place where I have to take time to process my grief. At those times, I often go back to the day that Reggie died. In such moments, I feel like I did something wrong and that my life is more difficult than the average American.

When my triggers cause me to get that emotional, I need that time to do a Thought Map to make sure that I know where the feelings are coming from and can process them accordingly so that I don't react. That is how you should proceed in similar situations, too.

Now it's time for you to complete this category (Trigger):

Identify & Organize	Power of Choice
Core Connections Leave this blank for now, we will come back to it.	Leave this blank for now, we will come back to it.
Triggers • List the triggers in your Thought Map, these are external factors that are causing a reaction.	• Choose what you are going to do with your triggers. Use Choice Opportunities provided.
Grief • List the loss in your Thought Map here	
Trauma • List any trauma from your Thought Map here, you can leave items blank if needed	
Negative Thoughts Rating (Belief) • List the negative thought here and _____ /10 rate how much you believe them. _____ /10 _____ /10	
Behaviors/Choices • Do you have any behaviors or choices in your Thought Map?	
Anxiety/Worry Rating (Time Spent) • What worries came up, and rate _____ /10 how much time do you spend? _____ /10 _____ /10	
Injustices • Write down any injustice that came up in your Thought Map	
Spiritual Conflict • Write down any spiritual conflict that came up in your Thought Map	
Addiction	

- Write down any addiction that may
  have come up in your Thought Map.

Repeat this process for each of your identified triggers by completing the Choice Opportunity worksheets attached to this lesson. Give yourself the time needed to fully process each of them. Completing Choice Opportunities every factor that you identified in element two (Identify and Organize) can increase your insight into how you will move forward in a more positive way towards your personal goals.

Once you have established the Power of Choice in relation to your triggers, you have freed up some of your mental energy and are on your way to taking control of the trigger(s). You can now take the steps towards processing the remaining categories in your metaphorical file cabinet, allowing yourself to understand and continue to work on the central thought identified in the Thought Map.

Can you see why it is helpful to separate external triggers from your thoughts and feelings? You can write about it here after you've completed the following Choice Opportunity.

_____

_____

_____

_____

_____

Choice Opportunity: Evaluate Triggers

Expected Outcome: Process the triggers with rationale thoughts and understanding the feeling with identification of thoughts.

Choose to recatagorize into another section, reframe thinking, or release the trigger.

Instructions: Step 1-Describe the situation in detail below.

Describe Event in Detail:

Step 2- Record the Thoughts heard in the situation. WHAT I FELT/HEARD--	STEP 3-Rate how much you believe the thought in your head and your heart. Scale of 0 (None) -10 (Totally)	Reflect and Identify	RE-Catagorize, Reframe, or Release
	/10 /10		
	/10 /10		
	/10 /10		
	/10 /10		
	/10 /10		

Author: Cristi Bundukamara

Grief

"Unfortunately, you need to feel the pain of grief." - 𝒟𝓇. ℬ

You are now ready to complete the second category in Element 3 (Power of Choice). So, let's continue working on this third element by taking that next step. You will now look at your Grief as identified and filed in Element 2 (Identify and Organize). Consider these important points when working through this section:

- You have the Power of Choice to choose what you are going to do with your grief, regardless of the type or source of the grief.

- I am going to challenge you to fully feel and process the pain of your grief in order to experience growth. I like to think of this as controlled grief.

Controlled Grief- choosing to take the time to grieve when it comes to the surface, but in a controlled manner. Allowing yourself a predetermined time to grieve.

Example: A Boiling Teapot Theory.

If you let a little steam (grief) out at a time, then with time, the intensity and frequency of it will decrease. The relief of pressure will also keep the grief manageable, allowing you to function and live your life.

- We are often taught that grief is a process that ends in the acceptance of a loss. In my experience, I have not found this to be true. Trying to obtain "acceptance" only leads to artificially accepting the loss, resulting in suppression of the pain.

- I cannot stress the importance of devoting enough time to grieving, but, conversely, do not let it be all-consuming for an extended period of time. You have to work on it in chunks. This is where **CONTROLLED GRIEF** is instrumental as a tool to manage and process your grief. Remember, you have control.

- If you let the grief impact your life in an overwhelming way, you are missing out on life, and more importantly, you are creating negative thinking pathways in your brain. These negative pathways become more difficult to reverse and overcome with time. It is not impossible but does become more difficult so you should try to avoid it.

- Do not hide your grief away. Learn to bring it out in a controlled manner. You are often aware when grief is present. During these times, allow yourself to grieve. Bring it to the forefront and feel the pain for a controlled period. When you are done grieving, return the pain to its place in your metaphorical file cabinet.

- Suppressing grief for long periods of time is not effective or healthy. However, suppressing it at limited times until you can deal with it in a controlled way might be appropriate.

- Know and understand that everyone experiences grief. Finding the positive in your grief should be your goal. The positive in some cases may be that you will eventually be a stronger person who can help others in the grief process.

Dr. B's Journey

Unfortunately, I am an expert in grief. I lost my 13-year-old son Johnny in a drowning accident in 2005 and I lost my son Reggie to a rare neurodegenerative disorder called DRPLA in 2016. I will likely lose my husband and daughter to the same disorder. When I say there is no magic formula for processing grief, that you literally have to sit with the pain, I am speaking from experience.

The importance of using the Mentally STRONG Method is that there are more categories that will get confused and enmeshed with your grief and it can become unbearable. I often hear other parents that have lost children say their lives are over. They no longer feel joy or purpose. It doesn't have to be that way though and I know your child in eternity does not want that for you. I can honestly say, it has been very hard for me, but I do have joy and purpose in my life. If you struggle with grief, continue to follow me on social media. Let's show the world that we can be Mentally STRONG.

Now it's time for you to complete this category (Grief):

Identify & Organize	Power of Choice
Core Connections Leave this blank for now, we will come back to it.	Leave this blank for now, we will come back to it.
Triggers • List the triggers in your Thought Map, these are external factors that are causing a reaction.	• Choose what you are going to do with your triggers. Use Choice Opportunities provided.
Grief • List the loss in your Thought Map here	• Use a Choice Opportunity to choose how you are going to work through the grief in your Thought Map.
Trauma • List any trauma from your Thought Map here, you can leave items blank if needed	
Negative Thoughts **Rating (Belief)** • List the negative thought here and rate how much you believe them. _____/10 _____/10 _____/10	
Behaviors/Choices • Do you have any behaviors or choices in your Thought Map?	
Anxiety/Worry **Rating (Time Spent)** • What worries came up, and rate how much time do you spend? _____/10 _____/10 _____/10	
Injustices • Write down any injustice that came up in your Thought Map	
Spiritual Conflict • Write down any spiritual conflict that came up in your Thought Map	
Addiction • Write down any addiction that may have come up in your Thought Map.	

www.mentallystrong.com    Mentally STRONG™   Author: Cristi Bundukamara

103

Repeat this process for each of your identified areas of grief by completing the Choice Opportunity worksheets attached to this lesson. Give yourself the time needed to fully process each of them. Completing Choice Opportunities for every factor that you identified in element two (Identify and Organize) can increase your insight into how you will move forward in a more positive way towards your personal goals.

Once you have established the Power of Choice in relation to your grief, you have once again freed up some of your mental energy and are on your way to taking control of your grief. You can now take the steps towards processing the remaining categories in your metaphorical file cabinet, allowing yourself to continue to understand and work on the central thought identified in the Thought Map.

Can you see why it is helpful to separate grief from your thoughts and feelings? You can write about it here after you've completed the following Choice Opportunities.

_____

_____

_____

_____

Choice Opportunity: Controlled Grief

Expected outcome: Understand the nature of grief and how to use "controlled grief" to maintain a purpose and level of functioning in the midst of intense emotional and disabling pain from a significant loss that you've experienced.

What is the grief process? We are taught that grief is a process that ends with the acceptance of a loss. We have been told to move on or to get over it, and to ultimately accept it. This is not an accurate recommendation, however. Grief is painful and a loss that deserves recognition, processing, and time. From my experience working with many who have experienced grief, trying to obtain this end goal of "acceptance" only leads to artificially accepting the loss. It does nothing more than suppress the painful and intense feelings coming from that loss, and is also why unsurmountable grief can arise and interfere with future decision making and your Personal Vision.

It's essential to acknowledge that loss and grief are not in line with what you want in your life and that the loss you experienced is contradictory to your Personal Vision. I cannot stress enough the importance of devoting time to grieving, but, at the same time, also advise you to not let it be consuming for a long period of time. This is where controlled grief is instrumental as a tool to manage and process the grief.

If you let the grief be overwhelmingly impactful in your life, you will be not only missing out on life, but more importantly, you will be creating negative thought pathways in your brain. These negative pathways become more difficult to reverse over time, and then overcoming them is more challenging (although not impossible).

Step 1: From your Thought Map, list the grief that you have identified and the need you are facing with regard to the loss: recent grief, delayed grief, anticipatory grief.

1. _____

2. _____

3. _____

4. _____

Step 2: Follow the doctor's orders in the Controlled Grief prescription. Appropriate processing of grief over time (with the use of controlled grief) should result in a decreased intensity of the feelings (from grief) and a lower frequency with which the grief affects you.

Mentally STRONG™ 1
R PATIENT'S NAME _____ AGE _____
ADDRESS _____ DATE _____
Controlled Grief
___ min ___x/wk
SUBSTITUTION PERMISSIBLE _____ M.D.

Cristi Bundukamara, Ed.D, PMHNP-BC

- Identify the grief that is affecting your mood. Sit with a picture, memorabilia, or cherished item from your loved one or associated with the loss that you experienced. Feel the pain of your loss with intention (to remember and honor the loss).

- Feel the range of feelings associated with this loss. Be sure to express your thoughts and talk to the person (as if they were there) or about the loss. Get all of your thoughts out with honesty and clarity.

- PRN: when intense or unexpected memories emerge with triggers, take time for controlled grief, then return to your normal activities.

- On special occasions or an anniversary, take the whole day off.

Step 3: Create a plan for controlled grief as ordered. Set aside the time for yourself and allow yourself to grieve. It's critical for your forward growth. Outline your plan while considering the following:

_____

_____

- Suppressing grief for long periods of time is not effective or healthy.
- Suppressing your grief until after the workday ends might be appropriate.
- Grief is not about acceptance. You will always feel the loss.
- **There will be pain and other feelings, too. However, in time, the frequency and intensity of your grief will decrease.**

Choice Opportunity: Emotional Teapot Theory

Expected outcome: Understand the negative results of stuffing or not processing your emotions or feelings. You will also learn how to understand your emotions and feelings better. **THIS IS NOT FOR ANXIETY:** Ruminating on your worry can worsen your anxiety (so don't do it).

A boiling teapot is a good way to see the effects of your feelings when you refuse to recognize, process, or feel those feelings from your life experiences.

Your feelings, like the boiling water, need to escape from the vessel periodically. That is why there is a relief valve in the design of the teapot. What happens if you block that release valve in the teapot? The same will happen to you if you block those feelings.

You are no different than the teapot. You need to release your feelings. You cannot stuff or bottle them up over an extended period of time in a healthy manner.

The practice of refusing to acknowledge, feel, or process your feelings will change you, and will have an impact on who you are. It will also have a negative impact on you as a person in many areas: emotional, mental, physical health, and within your social life. It is vital to recognize when you are stuffing your feelings. It happens when you choose to avoid your feelings. Now is the time to recognize and change that behavior and practice.

What feelings are your refusing to feel with stuffing, blocking, or ignoring the feelings?

_____

_____

_____

_____

What do you think will happen if you continually refuse to feel these feelings?

_____

_____

_____

_____

What could happen if you start acknowledging and feeling these feelings?

Mental   Emotional   Physical   Spiritual

How will you release the pressure in your teapot and begin to let off the steam? How will you feel those feelings or express yourself in healthy ways to improve your mental health?

_____

_____

_____

What choices will you make to let go (in a safe way) and to experience the feelings and be heard?

_____

_____

_____

Trauma

"Trauma is anything that changes your reality. Process the trauma in your life to minimize the impact it has on your choices, now and in the future."

- Dr. B

You are now ready to complete the third category in Element 3 (Power of Choice). So, let's keep working on this element by taking this next step. You will now look at your personal Trauma as identified and filed in Element 2 (Identify and Organize). Keep in mind the following as you work through this step:

- If you have experienced trauma, know and understand that it is not right and it is not fair. To get stronger, you must acknowledge the effects it's had on your life so that it does not continue to impact your mental or physical health.
- Acknowledging trauma may be a lifetime journey, but it is very important. The trauma you've experienced has altered your life, beliefs, perspectives, sense of security, coping strategies, actions, and behaviors. Both you and your dreams have been changed as a result of the trauma you've been through.
- Recognizing that trauma has made an imprint on and changed you is crucial. It is also vital to understand that this trauma does not complete or define you.
- The full processing of your trauma should result in a decrease of its effects over time (with more intensity and frequency in terms of this processing).

Dr. B's Journey:

As a psychiatric nurse practitioner, I hear horrific stories of trauma all the time. The reality is that the more chronic and complex the trauma, the more distressing it is to the brain and the harder it is for the person to make sense of a perceived safe and happy world. Early in my self-development, I denied trauma. I was date-raped at the age of 14 by a man who was 19 years old. Like most victims of date-rape, I blamed myself for it and did not identify that experience as trauma. Compared to the horrific abuse I have heard from some of my clients, I almost feel guilty saying that this experience was trauma. But, when it comes to trauma, it is not about comparing. It's about identifying how the experience (the rape in my case) impacted my personal development. Further, it's about how I make choices to acknowledge and process that trauma and find the strength to move past it.

This incident negatively changed my perception of men (which was already a complicated issue for me). I did not have a father until I was nine years old when my mom re-married, so I didn't have much to pull from early on. My stepdad tried to love me, but I didn't feel it. He often told us (his daughters) that men were only interested in sex and could not be trusted. That was the basis of my belief about men which was further confirmed when I was date-raped after my first romantic interest in a man.

Besides confirming what my stepdad had warned me about, being raped also negatively impacted my thoughts and mood by reinforcing some of my negative self-talk. It told me that I must be fat and ugly. If I was beautiful, it wouldn't have happened, and he would have loved me. It also showed me that I was not smart. A smart girl wouldn't have been raped or have put herself in that situation. I have acknowledged (and continue to acknowledge) how this trauma has impacted my perception, thoughts, and mood.

I had to take the next step, processing the trauma, which is similar to processing grief. I grieved my loss. In this case, I lost the perception that intimate relationships are *safe. Just like feeling the pain of grief, we have to feel whatever emotions come up for us when we are grieving trauma. For me, it caused sadness, and when compounded with other things, it can sometimes cause depression. This is not a onetime process, but the more you acknowledge and process (similar to grief), the less often you will need to. The more compounded and complex the trauma, the more time you will need (again, just like with grief).*

As the final step, you will find your strength. Finding your strength may be choosing to seek professional help or it may be something else. Trauma can change our brain chemistry and cause PTSD (which can be treated). It's likely that I unconsciously chose a helping profession as my strength. There is healing in helping. It is called altruism. Finding your strength is an individual thing. You will find it on your own. I can't do it for you, but I believe we can all find our strength, through insight and choice.

Complete the category (Trauma) for yourself:

Identify & Organize	Power of Choice
Core Connections Leave this blank for now, we will come back to it.	Leave this blank for now, we will come back to it.
Triggers • List the triggers in your Thought Map, these are external factors that are causing a reaction.	• Choose what you are going to do with your triggers. Use Choice Opportunities provided.
Grief • List the loss in your Thought Map here	• Use a Choice Opportunity to choose how you are going to work through the grief in your Thought Map.
Trauma • List any trauma from your Thought Map here, you can leave items blank if needed	• Use the provided Choice Opportunities to make choices regarding your trauma.
Negative Thoughts Rating (Belief) • List the negative thought here and rate how much you believe them. ____/10 ____/10 ____/10	
Behaviors/Choices • Do you have any behaviors or choices in your Thought Map?	
Anxiety/Worry Rating (Time Spent) • What worries came up, and rate how much time do you spend? ____/10 ____/10 ____/10	
Injustices • Write down any injustice that came up in your Thought Map	
Spiritual Conflict • Write down any spiritual conflict that came up in your Thought Map	
Addiction • Write down any addiction that may have come up in your Thought Map.	

Repeat this process for each of your identified areas of trauma by completing the Choice Opportunity worksheets attached to this lesson. Give yourself the time needed to fully process each of them. Completing Choice Opportunities for every factor that you identified in element two (Identify and Organize) can increase your insight into how you will move forward in a more positive way towards your personal goals.

Once you have established the Power of Choice in relation to your trauma, you have once again freed up some of your mental energy and are on your way to taking control of your trauma. You can now take the steps towards processing the remaining categories in your metaphorical file cabinet, allowing yourself to continue to understand and work on the central thought identified in the Thought Map.

Can you see why it is helpful to separate trauma from your thoughts and feelings? You can write about it here after you've completed the following Choice Opportunities.

_____

_____

_____

_____

_____

Choice Opportunity: Comfortable in Your Story

Expected outcome: To acquire the ability to share your story with a sense of comfort when telling it to others without extreme distress, discomfort, shame or overwhelming emotions.

What does your story include: ○ Grief   ○ Trauma
                                 ○ Bad Choices   ○ Injustices
                                 ○ Addiction   ○ _____

1. Tell your story: _____

   _____

   _____

   _____

   _____

   _____

   _____

2. Identify thoughts, feelings, or emotions that emerge: _____

   _____

   _____

   _____

3. I coped by: _____

   _____

   _____

4. The following people helped: _____

_____

_____

5. Who or what do you blame: _____

_____

_____

6. How this changed your life: _____

_____

_____

7. How you forgave and whom you forgave: _____

_____

_____

8. How you overcame: _____

_____

_____

9. Steps you can take to become more comfortable with your story: _____

_____

_____

This is your Choice Opportunity to be Mentally STRONG™ and comfortable in your story!

Learn more about *The Mentally STRONG Method*: **1-800-55-STRONG ~ www.mentallystrong.com**

Choice Opportunity: Letter to Your Younger Self

Expected Outcome: Provides an opportunity to talk with yourself when you were younger while being abused, taken advantage of, or hurt when you were vulnerable. The aim of this exercise is to allocate the misplaced feelings and ownership of guilt, shame and blame on the offender and others, and remove it from you.

Instructions: Answer the following questions.

Dear _____(me),

1. If you could release the blame or guilt of the past, what would that look and feel like? _____

   _____

2. If you could release the guilt of the past, what would that look and feel like?

   _____

   _____

3. If you could release the shame of the past, what would that look and feel like?

   _____

   _____

4. If you were talking to a child who is the same age as you were in your situation, what would you say to them? _____

   _____

   _____

This is your Choice Opportunity to be Mentally STRONG™ in yourself.

Negative Thought

"You have to know yourself to love yourself" *– Dr. B*

You are now ready to complete the fourth category in Element 3 (Power of Choice). You will now look at your Negative Thought(s) as identified and filed in Element 2 (Identify and Organize). As you do so, consider the following:

- It is very likely that your negative thoughts started in the past. Hovering in this negative place is easy for you because you have become comfortable reverting to the same negative thoughts (but don't fall for that comfort).

- Challenge yourself to create more positive thoughts so that you can begin rebuilding positive pathways. During times of duress, our brains move towards negative thought pathways because it's the easiest for us, but doing so can lead to blame, guilt, and shame (so turn towards the positive).

- As part of this category, you will want to significantly reduce your belief rating scale as noted in element 2 (Identify/Organize) so that you can stop the negative thoughts from taking over your thinking, choices, and behaviors.

- It is nearly impossible to eradicate ALL negative thoughts, but you can decrease the frequency, intensity, and influence of them.

- It will take practice and repetition, but you can find new (positive) thoughts and strengthen the ability to stop the negative thoughts from taking over.

- As part of this category, you will be working to break the cycle of your automatic regression to the past. As such, it is important to replace your negative thoughts with positive thoughts when you recognize this pattern of negative thinking.

- You must do the work to rationalize your thoughts and consider the accuracy and validity of the negative thoughts that you are saying to and about yourself. Reframe and refocus these thoughts into positive thoughts (be kind to yourself).

- Negative thought patterns are theoretical neuropathways. In order to reverse them, you must create new positive pathways.

Dr. B's Journey:

This category is a little bit different. Here, I will have you rate your negative thoughts. So often, people have negative thoughts that they mostly believe, and it can be hard to change those negative thoughts into positive thoughts. Therefore, I am going to have you do a rating scale.

I have a few negative thoughts that persist. For example, I shared with you earlier that I believed that I was not smart since I was a child. In my teen years, I would have rated that negative thought as a 6-8, meaning 6 on a good day and 8 on a bad day. After years of practicing positive thoughts and finding my strength, I now know that I am very smart in many ways. On a good day, I do not believe that I am not smart, and even on a bad day after failure, I only rate it at a 2 and can move on rather quickly.

Another persistent negative thought that I have is that I often say that **I can't** do something when, in fact, **I can** (and likely will). For example, sometimes the fact that I am a caregiver becomes overwhelming for me and I feel like **I can't** do it anymore. When this happens, I reframe the situation and I tell myself that perhaps I can't do it perfectly, but **I can** do it!

Sometimes I also say, "**this won't work**" or prophesize that something will go **wrong**. When I find myself in those situations, I again begin to reframe them. I tell myself instead that it **will** work and think about what can go **right instead**.

What we think about ourselves is another strong contributing, and often unhealthy, thought, particularly for women. We often have negative thoughts related to our weight and appearance. When we do, we tell ourselves negative things that we would never say to other people. If I begin to think that way, I ask myself if I would ever say that thought to my children. If I wouldn't say it to my child, I should never say it to myself.

Complete this category (Negative Thought) for yourself:

Identify & Organize	Power of Choice
Core Connections Leave this blank for now, we will come back to it.	Leave this blank for now, we will come back to it.
Triggers • List the triggers in your Thought Map, these are external factors that are causing a reaction.	• Choose what you are going to do with your triggers. Use Choice Opportunities provided.
Grief • List the loss in your Thought Map here	• Use a Choice Opportunity to choose how you are going to work through the grief in your Thought Map.
Trauma • List any trauma from your Thought Map here, you can leave items blank if needed	• Use the provided Choice Opportunities to make choices regarding your trauma.
Negative Thoughts **Rating (Belief)** • List the negative thought here and rate how much you believe them. ___/10 ___/10 ___/10	• Use the Choice Opportunities provided to help make choices about your negative thoughts.
Behaviors/Choices • Do you have any behaviors or choices in your Thought Map?	
Anxiety/Worry **Rating (Time Spent)** • What worries came up, and rate how much time do you spend? ___/10 ___/10 ___/10	
Injustices • Write down any injustice that came up in your Thought Map	
Spiritual Conflict • Write down any spiritual conflict that came up in your Thought Map	
Addiction • Write down any addiction that may have come up in your Thought Map.	

You are doing some solid work here. Repeat this process for each of your identified negative thoughts by completing the Choice Opportunity worksheets attached to this lesson. Give yourself the time needed to fully process each of them. Completing Choice Opportunities for every factor that you identified in element two (Identify and Organize) can increase your insight into how you will move forward in a more positive way towards your personal goals.

Once you have established the Power of Choice in relation to your negative thoughts, you have once again freed up some of your mental energy and are on your way to taking control of your negative thinking. You can now take the steps towards processing the remaining categories in your metaphorical file cabinet, allowing yourself to continue to understand and work on the central thought identified in the Thought Map.

Can you see why it is helpful to separate negative thought from your thoughts and feelings? You can write about it here after you've completed the following Choice Opportunities.

_____

_____

_____

_____

_____

Choice Opportunity: Distorted Thinking Types

Expected Outcome: Your identification of maladaptive thinking that is impacting your mental health and delaying progress towards your Personal Vision.

Step 1: From the list below, select your frequently used distorted thinking types/style.

_____ **All or Nothing Thinking**

Definition: Thinking in extremes, you are either a success or a failure

Example: Making opposing statements about the same concern. "I am 100% committed to weight loss and will do it ALL to achieve." While also stating "Weight doesn't matter, I am doing nothing to achieve the goal therefore I will eat ice cream and watch TV all day."

_____ **Blanket statements**

Definition: The use of overgeneralizing statements that cover all options but usually on one of the two extremes. A metaphorical blanket statement about options or actions.

Examples: Using absolutes within the statement. "everything", "always", "everyone", "nothing". Everyone is upsetting me. Nothing is going right. Everything sucks.

_____ **Negative thought patterns**

Definition: Disqualifying the positive statements and options for the situation, usually without even taking the time to consider the positive choices.

Examples: My glass is ½ empty thinking. Nothing will ever go right. Nobody cares. It is a sunny day but you only notice the potholes on the street.

_____ **Assumptions**

Definition: Assuming that you know what others are thinking, feeling, or how they will respond to a question or inquiry.

Example: I already know that my mom won't let me go out with friends so why even bother asking.

_____ **Catastrophizing**

Definition: Blowing the situation out of proportion and making it the worst-case scenario.

Example: I am currently only working part-time so we are going to starve to death

_____ **Blaming**

Definition: Blaming yourself or taking responsibility for something that wasn't 100% your fault. Blaming others for something that was your own doing without accepting any responsibility.

Example: It is the spoon's fault that I am fat!

Step 2: Of the Distorted thinking style that you selected, rank them from the most frequently used (1) to the least frequently used (6).

1. _____

2. _____

3. _____

4. _____

5. _____

6. _____

Step 3: Identify the highest ranked distorted thinking style:

_____

Complete the Choice Opportunity worksheet identified as the distorted thinking style.

    After completing the worksheet identified, go to step 4.

Step 4: What is the opposite of that distorted thinking style:

_____

Step 5: Develop a plan to incorporate a positive strategy with thinking.

_____

_____

_____

_____

This is YOUR choice opportunity to be  with your thoughts.

Learn more about *The Mentally STRONG Method*: 1-800-55-STRONG ~ www.mentallystrong.com

Choice Opportunity: Balanced Thinking

Expected Outcome: Balance the All -or- Nothing thinking with a balanced perspective.

Step 1-List your all or nothing thoughts on each side of the arrow.
Step 2-Create one statement incorporating the two extremes to gain a sense of awareness with a balanced perspective.

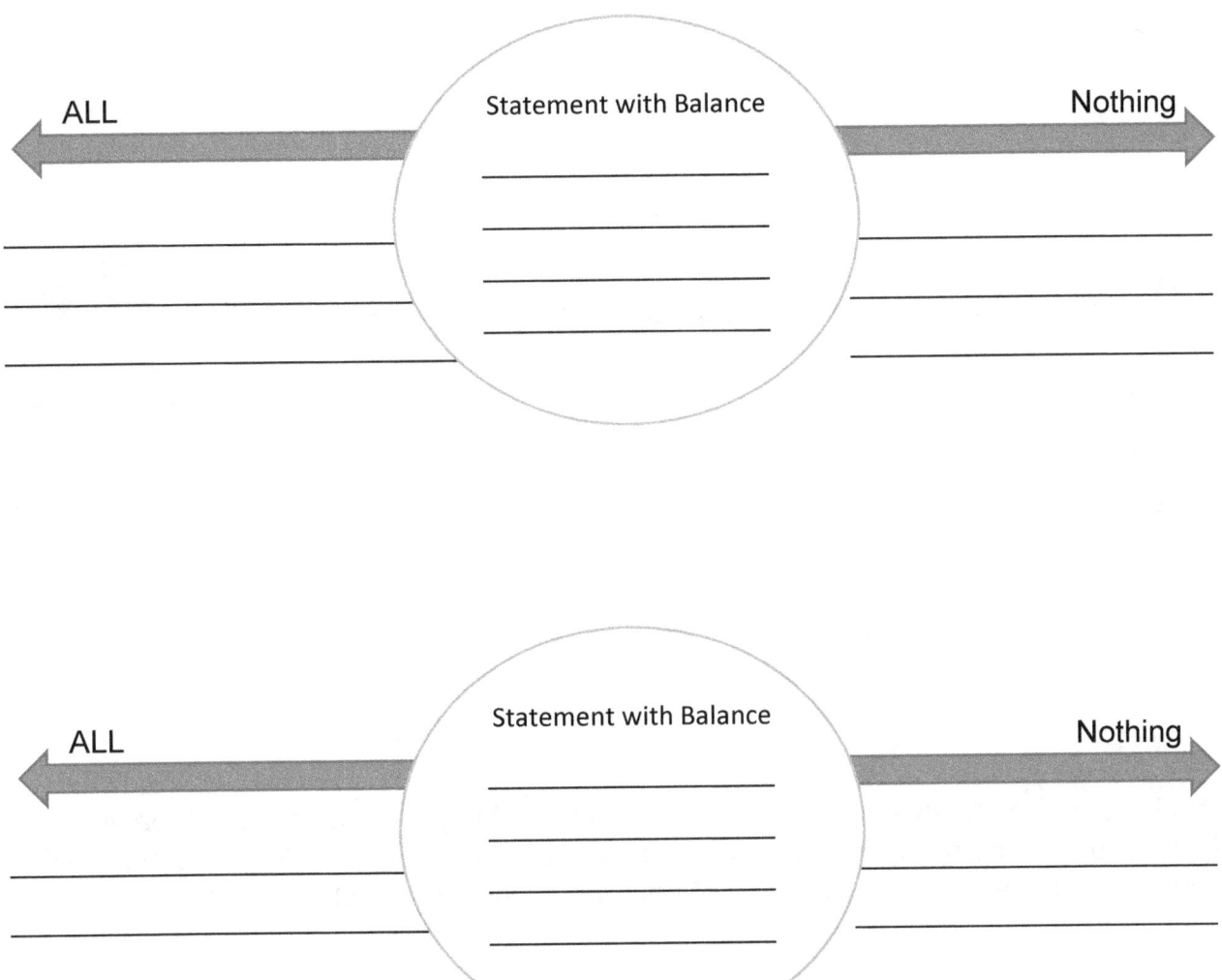

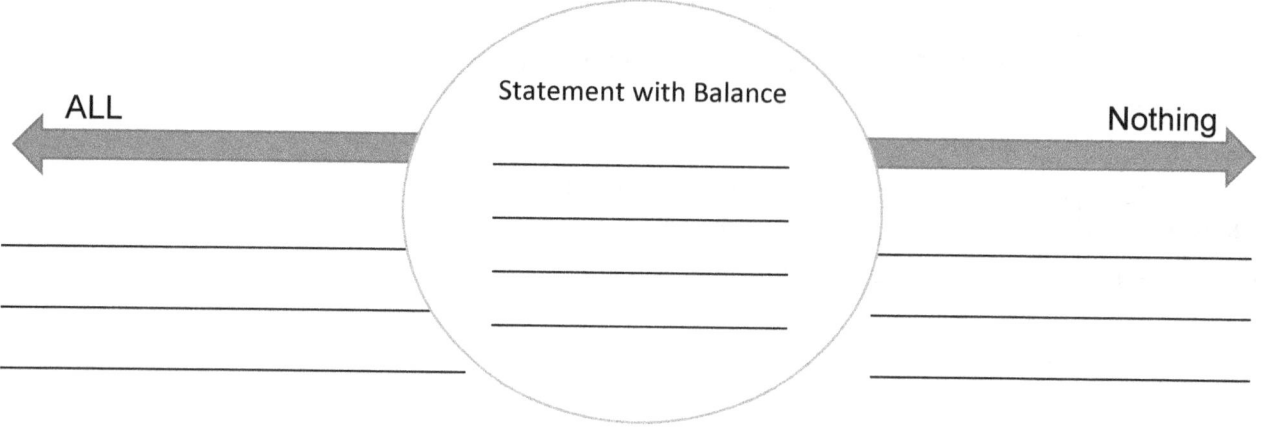

This is your opportunity to choose to live and stay within your statement with balance. When you find yourself going toward either extreme, then you need to gain a sense of awareness and allow your statement of balance to bring you back to center.

This is your *Choice Opportunity* to be Mentally STRONG™ and balanced!

Choice Opportunity: Be Specific

Expected Outcome: Eliminate the use of overgeneralized statements and replace them with facts and details in accurate and positive statements.

Step 1: Complete the sentences below with statements you made during The Mentally STRONG Method session.

Everyone is _____.

I always _____.

Nothing is _____.

Everything is _____.

Everybody is _____.

_____.

_____.

_____.

_____.

_____.

Step 2: Identify the overgeneralization in the statements above by circling what makes the statement an overgeneralization.

Step 3: Further explore and break down the specifics contained in the blanket statement. Include the who, what, when, where details that are being overgeneralized in the statements.

(Who-Name) _____ is _____.

I always (When) _____.

Nothing (What-Name) is _____.

Everything (What-Name) _____.

Everybody (Who-Name) is_____.

_____.

_____.

_____.

_____.

_____.

Learn more about *The Mentally STRONG Method*: 1-800-55-STRONG ~ www.mentallystrong.com

When you rephrased the statement without the overgeneralization, did you have a new feeling or experience a change in emotion?

If yes, then consider exploring that feeling if it is negative or disturbing. If no, then proceed.

Step 4: Consider why are you using overgeneralizations?

_____

_____

_____

Step 5: Is there an avoidance or defensive behavior in choosing to overgeneralize as an excuse to changing your behaviors?

_____

_____

_____

Choose to reflect on the overgeneralizations and re-frame, reclassify, or release the blanket statement with new details and accuracy.

Step 6: Pick one overgeneralization listed above. Give 5-10 specific examples of when this statement was not true or accurate.

_____   _____

_____   _____

_____   _____

_____   _____

_____   _____

This is a perfect example of when our choices are negative thoughts and create negative pathways which are easy to revert back to in times of weakness or chaos. This is your opportunity to recognize your use of blanket statements and to change your thinking and processing of the options available to your current problems, conflicts, or struggles.

This is YOUR choice opportunity to be Mentally STRONG™ and specific!

Learn more about *The Mentally STRONG Method*: **1-800-55-STRONG ~ www.mentallystrong.com**

Choice Opportunity: Benefit Analysis - Negative Thoughts

Expected Outcome: Self-analysis of your thoughts, the situation, and consideration of the options available to make the choice to change to positive thinking.

The purpose of a benefit analysis is to consider all of the factors in a situation, and to decide based on the facts disclosed during the investigation of the factors (for the relevant components impacting the situation). When you have areas of your behavior or personality that are maladaptive (and not supporting your Personal Vision), it is important to figure out why you continue to do the same things repeatedly expecting a different outcome. If you can understand the motivation, even subconsciously, you can make a more conscious effort to change your behaviors with different choices.

Step 1: Identify and list the negative thoughts affecting you.

_____ .

_____ .

_____ .

Step 2: What benefit do you gain by maintaining the current way of thinking and/or behaving?

_____

_____

_____

Step 3: What negative outcomes do you gain by maintaining the current way of thinking and/or behaving?

_____

_____

_____

Step 4: What is the likely mental, emotional, physical, or spiritual consequences of your current thoughts and behaviors? List them in each area where applicable*.

Mental	Emotional	Physical	Spiritual

Step 5: Why do you think you are continuing to have the patterns of negative

thoughts that include putting yourself down and thinking or expecting less from yourself?

_____

_____

_____

_____

Step 6: What are the possible outcomes with a change in the actions or behaviors?
- What are the benefits if you are committed to changing your anxiety, actions, behaviors, or thoughts?
- What is the benefit to not changing your anxiety, actions, behaviors, or thoughts?
- What is the benefit of refusing to change your anxiety, actions, behaviors, or thoughts?

Committed to Change	No Change	Refuse to Change
%	%	%

What is the likely percentage of you choosing to change your actions/behaviors and way of thinking? Indicate those numbers in the area above.

Step 7: What is your plan to change? List specific actions, changes, and include details.

_____

_____

_____

_____

_____

This is your *Choice Opportunity* to be Mentally STRONG™ in positive thinking!

Learn more about *The Mentally STRONG Method*: **1-800-55-STRONG ~ www.mentallystrong.com**

*The Mentally STRONG Method with Choice Opportunities© Author: Cristi Bundukamara – not for reproduction/distribution

Choice Opportunity: Fact Collecting

Expected Outcome: Eliminate the use of assumptions and increase communication to gather the facts needed to make decisions or to process a situation.

Assuming is common when communication is limited or avoided. One person will assume that they know what the other person is going to say, do, or want. Most often, they are incorrect. Typically, these thoughts are based on your fears and worst-case scenarios, following more negative thought patterns. Without clear methods of communication, the likelihood of making assumptions is high. This practice can lead to misunderstandings, errors in judgement, hurt feelings, and an increase in negative emotions.

Step 1: List assumptions or statements from your Mentally STRONG Method session where you identify that you may not know all the facts and are assuming.

Example: My best friend does not like me anymore because he isn't hanging out with me anymore!

_____ ❏ Factual

_____ ❏ Factual

_____ ❏ Factual

_____ ❏ Factual

_____ ❏ Factual

_____ ❏ Factual

How do you know that these statements are facts and not assumed facts?

_____

_____

Are you assuming something that hasn't been clearly communicated? Is it affecting your relationship with someone else? _____

_____

What other perspectives or alternative scenarios have you considered to the statement made?

Example: The friend just got a new job or girlfriend, or a family member has passed away. In the absence of communication, you jumped to a conclusion and assumed that the friend does not like you anymore. Communication can clear up the misunderstanding.

_____

_____

Learn more about *The Mentally STRONG Method*: 1-800-55-STRONG ~ www.mentallystrong.com

What percentage do you believe the assumption?

_____

_____

_____

What percentage do you want to believe OPPOSITE of the assumption?

_____

_____

_____

How will you remain Mentally STRONG if the assumption is true?

_____

_____

Select one assumption listed above- the one that you believe the most and is causing the most conflict internally and with others.

ASSUMPTION: _____

Evidence to support the assumption: _____

Communications attempted in the past:

_____

Plan for communication: _____

Will you discuss the issue and address the assumption? How are you going to make sure that your head and heart are open to listen to what the other person has to say?

_____

_____

How are you going to listen to the other person's truth cognitively and emotionally?

_____

_____

This is your *Choice Opportunity* to be Mentally STRONG™ and communicate.

Learn more about *The Mentally STRONG Method*: **1-800-55-STRONG ~ www.mentallystrong.com**

Choice Opportunity: Be Optimistic

Expected outcome: Eliminate catastrophizing thinking thereby allowing more effective options to be considered in the current situation (and in the future).

Catastrophizing is the thought pattern in which a person goes to the worst-case scenario and will own the tragedy accompanied by negative thoughts. This is worrying to an extreme. Exponential worry about the future is often hyper-focused on the potential negative outcomes and worst-case scenarios, without consideration for possible positive outcomes or reasons (it's not balanced).

Example: I know that the reason the bomb-cyclone snowstorm happened was because no one wants me to go on spring break with me and I will never be able to ever go again because I am too busy.

Acknowledge your tendency to worry exponentially or excessively about the future.

Identify an event/problem/issue that you are worried about the future outcome.

Describe in detail:

_____

_____

_____

_____

What are the possible actions in this scenario along with the percentage of occurrence?

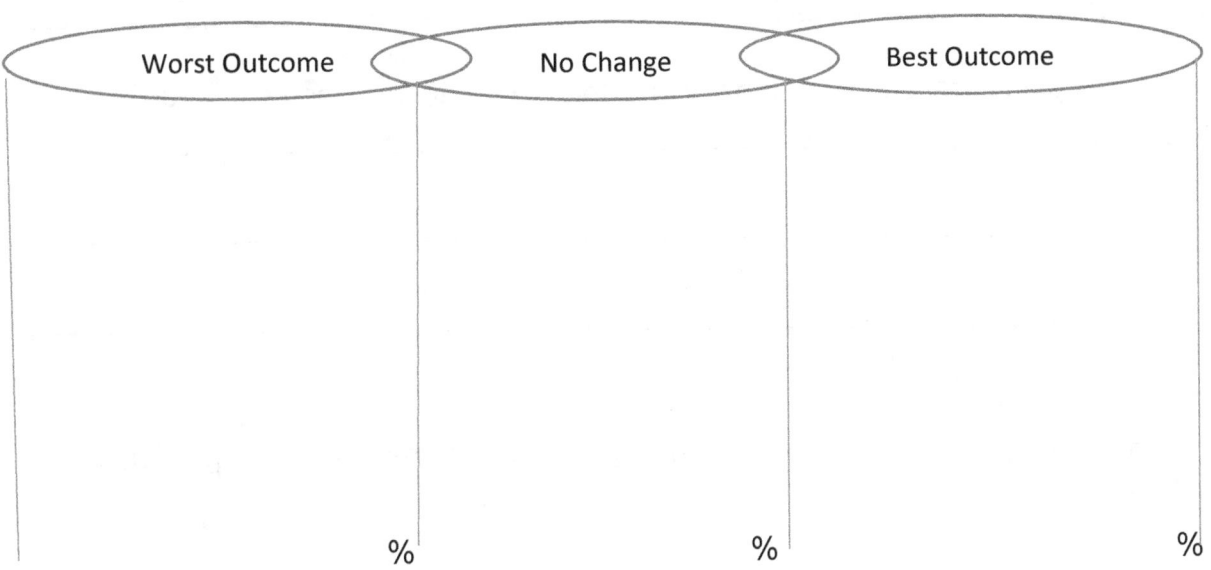

| Worst Outcome | No Change | Best Outcome |

%   %   %

What is an accurate perspective to state the facts in the situation?

_____

_____

_____

If the odds of the worst-case scenario are high, then you have a unique opportunity to prepare for the worst-case scenario.

While preparing for the worst, I hope that you will also continue to hope for the best until you know the outcome. I encourage you to remain positive with your thinking and decrease your worry over the unknown.

If the worst happens, you need to remain positive in those moments of increased stress and chaos. How are you going to maintain your mental strength and be Mentally STRONG in the event that the worst possible outcome actually happens?

_____

_____

_____

_____

How do you plan to rejoice and be grateful if the best outcome occurs instead?

_____

_____

_____

This is your *Choice Opportunity* to be Mentally STRONG™ and optimistic!

Choice Opportunity: Release Blame

Expected outcome: Eliminate the act of blaming and start living. You will become responsible and accountable for your actions. You will stop taking the blame from others (and putting it on yourself) where you have no responsibility or involvement. You will take ownership of your actions only when you are wrong and take the appropriate steps to make it right.

Briefly explain situation: _____

_____

_____

Who are you blaming? Yourself or others? Explain: _____

_____

_____

_____

List situations where you accepted the blame.

1. _____
2. _____
3. _____

Explain why you or someone else is to blame in the situation?

1. _____
2. _____
3. _____

STOP Take a moment to reflect on your answers. Pray and meditate on the answers provided.

- Are you being fair and just to yourself or others?
- Can you rationalize other important factors in the situation?

If you are not being fair/just to yourself by accepting the blame of others:

Learn more about *The Mentally STRONG Method*: **1-800-55-STRONG ~ www.mentallystrong.com**

Describe how you can forgive yourself and release the blame. This releasing will allow you to live in compassion, understanding, and give grace to yourself and others.

_____

_____

_____

_____

Describe how you can take mature responsibility for your actions: _____

_____

_____

_____

_____

Can you do the same if you blame others? _____

_____

_____

_____

_____

_____

_____

_____

This is your Choice Opportunity to be   Mentally STRONG™   and responsible!

Behaviors & Choices

"Choose boundaries in line with what you really want." - *Dr. B*

You are now ready to complete the next category in Element 3 (Power of Choice). You will now look at your Behaviors/Choices as identified and filed in Element 2 (Identify and Organize).

This section is about taking ownership around behaviors and choices. While working in this section, keep in mind that:

- It is important to acknowledge when your personal behaviors and choices are affecting how you act and are related to your identified thought or feeling. Sometimes our behaviors are ineffective in getting what we want or need, so we must adjust them. These are known as maladaptive behaviors.

> **Maladaptive Behaviors:** Maladaptive behaviors are actions that interfere with your ability to adjust to situations or adapt to changes occurring in your life. They are behaviors that do not serve your purpose. Often, maladaptive behaviors are a result of control issues that appear in our lives to help us in terms of coping. This need for control can become maladaptive.
>
> *Example:*
>
> *Choosing to ignore a problem as a coping strategy to life.*

- If you feel stuck and unable to see where you need to change, consider doing a Choice Opportunity for guidance.
- What are you gaining by continuing this behavior?
- Is there a secondary gain? This is a choice too.
- Choosing to do nothing is also a choice as well as continuing to do the same thing.

Dr. B's Journey:

I chose to start a business and hire caretakers for my daughter; however, I feel guilty about my choice sometimes. When I am feeling guilty or like I am not being a good mother, I need to take ownership of my decision. I can choose to make time to spend with my daughter after work or on the weekends (while still running the business).

As a married woman, I promised to stay with my husband for better or for worse. This is a choice that I have committed to. Sometimes, however, I struggle with being in a relationship that is not always rewarding or fulfilling for me (since I've become a caretake for my husband). There are choices that I can make to make it more manageable, though. I could choose to get a divorce, but I don't want to. There are other options. For example, I can take the time that I need for myself and find joy in other ways, and get help when caretaking becomes overwhelming for me.

Everything in life is a choice, but you may not always like your options. If you are in a relationship or situation where you are not being treated well, you are making a choice as to whether or not to stay in it. Make the choice(s) that align with your Personal Vision.

Now, it's time to complete this category (Behaviors & Choices):

Identify & Organize	Power of Choice
Core Connections Leave this blank for now, we will come back to it.	Leave this blank for now, we will come back to it.
Triggers • List the triggers in your Thought Map, these are external factors that are causing a reaction.	• Choose what you are going to do with your triggers. Use Choice Opportunities provided.
Grief • List the loss in your Thought Map here	• Use a Choice Opportunity to choose how you are going to work through the grief in your Thought Map.
Trauma • List any trauma from your Thought Map here, you can leave items blank if needed	• Use the provided Choice Opportunities to make choices regarding your trauma.
Negative Thoughts **Rating (Belief)** • List the negative thought here and rate how much you believe them. ____ /10 ____ /10 ____ /10	• Use the Choice Opportunities provided to help make choices about your negative thoughts.
Behaviors/Choices • Do you have any behaviors or choices in your Thought Map?	• Make choices about your behavior that are in line with your Personal Vision.
Anxiety/Worry **Rating (Time Spent)** • What worries came up, and rate how much time do you spend? ____ /10 ____ /10 ____ /10	
Injustices • Write down any injustice that came up in your Thought Map	
Spiritual Conflict • Write down any spiritual conflict that came up in your Thought Map	
Addiction • Write down any addiction that may have come up in your Thought Map.	

Repeat this process for each of your identified areas of behaviors/choices by completing the Choice Opportunity worksheets attached to this lesson. Give yourself the time needed to fully process each of them. Completing Choice Opportunities for every factor that you identified in element two (Identify and Organize) can increase your insight into how you will move forward in a more positive way towards your personal goals.

Once you have established the Power of Choice in relation to your behaviors/choices, you have once again freed up some of your mental energy and are on your way to taking control of your behaviors/choices. You can now take the steps towards processing the remaining categories in your metaphorical file cabinet, allowing yourself to continue to understand and work on the central thought identified in the Thought Map.

Can you see why it is helpful to separate negative behaviors and choices from your thoughts and feelings? You can write about it here after you've completed the following Choice Opportunities.

_____

_____

_____

_____

_____

Choice Opportunity: Benefit Analysis - Behaviors & Choices

Expected Outcome: Self-analysis of your thoughts, the situation, and consideration of the options available to take positive actions in relation to your behaviors and choices.

The purpose of a benefit analysis is to consider all of the factors in a situation and to make a decision based on the facts disclosed during the investigation (of the factors for the relevant components impacting the situation). When you have areas of your behavior or personality that are maladaptive and not supporting your personal vision, it is important to figure out why you continue to do the same things repeatedly expecting a different outcome. If you can understand the motivation, even subconsciously, you can make a more conscious effort to change your behaviors with different choices.

Step 1: Identify and list the behaviors and choices that are affecting you.

_____.

_____.

_____.

Step 2: What benefit do you gain by maintaining the current way of behaving?

_____

_____

_____

Step 3: What negative outcomes do you gain by maintaining the current way of behaving?

_____

_____

_____

Step 4: What is the likely mental, emotional, physical, or spiritual consequences of your current behaviors? List them in each area where applicable*.

Mental	Emotional	Physical	Spiritual

Step 5: Why do you think you are continuing to have these patterns of behavior with acting out or that are not serving your purpose?

_____

_____

_____

_____

Step 6: What are the possible outcomes with a change in the actions or behaviors?
- What are the benefits if you are committed to changing your anxiety, actions, behaviors, or thoughts?
- What is the benefit of not changing your behaviors, actions, behaviors, or thoughts?
- What is the benefit of refusing to change your anxiety, actions, behaviors, or thoughts?

Committed to Change	No Change	Refuse to Change
%	%	%

What is the likely percentage of you choosing to change your actions/behaviors and way of thinking? Indicate those numbers in the area above.

Step 7: What is your plan to change? List specific actions and changes and include details.

_____

_____

_____

_____

_____

This is your _Choice Opportunity_ to be   Mentally STRONG™   in your choices.

Learn more about _The Mentally STRONG Method_: **1-800-55-STRONG ~ www.mentallystrong.com**

Choice Opportunity: Healthy Boundaries

Expected outcome: Recognize behaviors and patterns to begin establishing a plan to create healthy boundaries. Boundaries are protective personal spaces, wants, and desires in our relationships with others, in the areas of physical, emotional, mental, and spiritual.

Telling all

Falling in love with a new acquaintance

Allowing other to disrespect you

Abuse

Self Pity

Making Choices based on what others want

Decisions to make others happy

Trusting Anyone

Preoccupied with a single relationship

Expecting others to fill your needs

Allowing others to take from you

Continued Victimizations

Not listening to yourself

Letting others define you

Inside the heart:

Saying no
Appropriate trust
Value true relationships
Know your worth
Honor yourself
Significance
Personal Values
Communicate wants
assertiveness
Defining Your Truth
Moving step by step in intimacy
Knowing who you are!
Protect yourself
Recognizing disrespect
Practice Self-Awareness
Focus on your own growth
Is it good for you?
Self Love
Respect others
Trusting Yourself
Only a little of yourself at a time
Appropriate Trust

Circle your unhealthy boundaries contained outside of the heart.

Identify additional unhealthy boundaries: _____

<u>Underline your healthy boundaries within the heart.</u>

Identify additional healthy boundaries: _____

Identify healthy boundaries you would like to work towards.

_____

How are your unhealthy boundaries hurting your heart?

_____

What choices do you need to make to protect yourself/make healthy choices?

_____

Learn more about *The Mentally STRONG Method*: 1-800-55-STRONG ~ www.mentallystrong.com

Choice Opportunity: Picture Perfect

Expected outcome: Understanding how the behavior of being perfect all the time, for everyone, in all situations, is an element of control and how it's not serving you well in attaining your personal visions.

Perfectionism is the belief that a state of perfection is attainable and sustainable across all areas of a person's life. This state of perfectionism is about always having to be perfect for everyone, all the time, and in all situations.

Sometimes there are self-imposed rules that impact multiple areas of your life. This application of self-imposed rules can create situations where the ability to vary or change is more difficult and involves greater stress. These self-imposed rules can be very stressful to maintain. It is unrealistic to put on the appearance of having no flaws or weaknesses.

Instructions: Answer the following questions:

1. In what areas of your life do you feel the need to be perfect? Work, school, home, community, other places?

   _____

   _____

2. Do you see this as a form of control?   Yes   No
   Do you know why you need to control these areas?
   Consider doing the "Choice Opportunity: Understanding Control" worksheet to determine areas where you need to control.

   _____

   _____

3. What would happen if there was something that was not perfect?

   _____

4. Would your anxiety and/or depression rating increase if there was something that was not perfect?

   _____

5. Is being perfect part of your identity and who you are?   Yes   No

6. Is this level of perfectionism an expectation of just yourself?   Yes   No

Learn more about *The Mentally STRONG Method*: 1-800-55-STRONG ~ www.mentallystrong.com

Others?   Yes   No

7. Is this expectation negatively impacting your relationships?   Yes   No

8. Is it possible to let go and not be perfect all the time for a day?   Yes   No
What would that look like?

_____

9. Reflect on the questions and answers above. How does your need to be perfect
impact these areas*?

Mental	Emotional	Physical	Spiritual
↓	↓	↓	↓

10. Identify one area where you do not have to be perfect.

_____

11. Develop a strategy to allow yourself to not be perfect in this identified area.

_____

_____

This is your Choice Opportunity to be Mentally STRONG™ in imperfection!

Choice Opportunity: Relationships are a Priority

Expected outcome: This is your opportunity to challenge yourself to view every person in your life as a relationship. You can choose to positively influence every person you encounter, and they can be a benefit to you.

Relationships are important at every level because people are important

Level 5: This involves every person you encounter. They may be the cashier at the grocery store or someone you meet at the park. You will only share with them what you want the world to know. These relationships are still important because you don't know how your interactions are impacting them, the environment, and everyone's purpose. Be the positive in the world. How can you promote positive energy and kindness to Level 5 Relationships?

_____

_____

Level 4: These are people you don't really trust (or don't know them well enough to trust), but you interact with them on a regular basis. I call these people acquaintances; this includes all the people you have contact with at work. An important boundary is to not share personal information that you are not willing to have judged or further shared. These (acquaintance) relationships are still important because you don't know how your interactions are impacting them, the environment, and everyone's purpose. Choose to empathize and practice kindness. How can you improve your kindness and positive energy in your day-to-day interactions?

_____

_____

_____

Level 3: These are people you trust with some personal things and a lot of practical things. These are the people I call friends. You are choosing to have a positive impact on their life and allowing them to have a positive impact on yours. Boundaries and expectations are important. Is there someone in this level that you need to identify boundaries or manage expectations for your own mental strength, describe: _____

_____

Is there someone in this group that might need help and you reaching out to them will make a difference in their life? _____

Level 2: These are people you trust with most things, including a lot of personal things. These are the people I call my good friends, some of them are family members. You are choosing to have a positive impact on their life and allowing them to have a positive impact on yours. Boundaries and expectations are important.

Level 1: These are people you trust with everything, including personal things. You need them and they need you. They could be your intimate partner. This could be some, but not all of your family members. It could be a small number, likely only one friend. These people can change based on the time in your life, but usually it has minimal change.

Are there areas where you could manage your expectations of your level 1 & 2 friends? This includes your intimate partner: _____

_____

_____

How can you have a balanced brain and avoid all or nothing thinking when it comes to your relationships?

_____

_____

_____

Remember: People can move in and out of the different levels. This can happen naturally due to time or location, or it could be a situation that may have caused discontent with the relationship. When you are practicing "all or nothing" thinking in relationships, you may be tempted to cut people out of your life intentionally, but this is unnecessary and can be harmful to both parties. Challenge yourself to manage your expectations in your relationships.

"Trust, forgive, and trust again"

- *Dr. B*

This is your opportunity to be Mentally STRONG™ in relationships.

Anxiety or Worry

"You have control of your anxiety and how it impacts you." - Dr. B

You are now ready to complete the next category in Element 3 (Power of Choice). You will now look at your Anxiety/Worry as identified and filed in Element 2 (Identify and Organize). As you do so, consider the following:

- Individuals, and some cultures, identify anxiety as a disorder in which you have no control. I am challenging this belief. You can choose to have control of your anxiety.

- Anxiety is a natural emotion in response to experience. It doesn't have to be all negative. It can be useful and productive, too.

- Anxiety is part of the "fight or flight" response related to danger or stress. But many times, anxiety becomes maladaptive and interferes with our progress and ability to function. Your challenge is to learn to appropriately manage your anxiety.

- It sounds very simple, to just take control of your anxiety, however, it can be extremely difficult. You are encouraged to try to control your anxiety and craft it to become a positive influence in your life.

Dr. B's Journey:

I struggle with decision making. My anxiety is usually associated with the fear of making a wrong choice. I often think extensively about my decisions (to an extreme), while I have a really hard time with details, augmenting my anxiety.

Some larger decisions have caused an even greater degree of anxiety for me. For example, I'm forced to make decisions related to my daughter's care on a regular basis. This activity conjures up feelings associated with decisions I've made in the past, particularly those that I made on the day that my son Reggie died. I still question whether or not I took him to the hospital at the right time. My fear of making the same mistake with my daughter causes an extreme amount of anxiety for me.

In my professional life, there are many decisions that involve risk which also fuel my anxiety. I'm a business owner and have to make many choices which have high risks in terms of time, money and more. These decisions impact not only myself and my family, but my employees and clients, too. The compromise or choice for me has been finding the balance between overly investigating and being stalled. Bad things will happen, but I can't let that fact (or my anxiety) stop me from making a decision at all.

Now it's time for you to complete this category (Anxiety & Worry)

Identify & Organize	Power of Choice
Core Connections Leave this blank for now, we will come back to it.	Leave this blank for now, we will come back to it.
Triggers • List the triggers in your Thought Map, these are external factors that are causing a reaction.	• Choose what you are going to do with your triggers. Use Choice Opportunities provided.
Grief • List the loss in your Thought Map here	• Use a Choice Opportunity to choose how you are going to work through the grief in your Thought Map.
Trauma • List any trauma from your Thought Map here, you can leave items blank if needed	• Use the provided Choice Opportunities to make choices regarding your trauma.
Negative Thoughts Rating (Belief) • List the negative thought here and rate how much you believe them. ____/10 ____/10 ____/10	• Use the Choice Opportunities provided to help make choices about your negative thoughts.
Behaviors/Choices • Do you have any behaviors or choices in your Thought Map?	• Make choices about your behavior that are in line with your Personal Vision.
Anxiety/Worry Rating (Time Spent) • What worries came up, and rate how much time do you spend? ____/10 ____/10 ____/10	• Use Choice Opportunities to help make choices regarding your anxiety.
Injustices • Write down any injustice that came up in your Thought Map	
Spiritual Conflict • Write down any spiritual conflict that came up in your Thought Map	
Addiction • Write down any addiction that may have come up in your Thought Map.	

Repeat this process for each of your identified areas of anxiety/worry by completing the Choice Opportunity worksheets attached to this lesson. Give yourself the time needed to fully process each of them. Completing Choice Opportunities for every factor that you identified in element two (Identify and Organize) can increase your insight into how you will move forward in a more positive way towards your personal goals.

Once you have established the Power of Choice in relation to your anxiety/worry, you have once again freed up some of your mental energy and are on your way to taking control of your anxiety/worry. You can now take the steps towards processing the remaining categories in your metaphorical file cabinet, allowing yourself to continue to understand and work on the central thought identified in the Thought Map.

Can you see why it is helpful to separate anxiety & worry from your thoughts and feelings? You can write about it here after you've completed the following Choice Opportunities.

_____

_____

_____

_____

_____

Choice Opportunity: Benefit Analysis- Anxiety & Worry

Expected Outcome: Self-analysis of your thoughts, the situation, and consideration of the options available to take positive actions in relation to your anxiety and worry.

The purpose of a benefit analysis is to consider all the factors in a situation and to make a decision based on the facts disclosed during the investigation (of the factors for the relevant components impacting the situation). When you have areas of your behavior or personality that are maladaptive and not supporting your personal vision, it is important to figure out why you continue to do the same things repeatedly expecting a different outcome. If you can understand the motivation, even subconsciously, you can make a more conscious effort to change your behaviors with different choices.

Step 1: Identify and list the anxiety and worry affecting you.

_____.

_____.

_____.

Step 2: What benefit do you gain by maintaining your current way of worrying?

_____

_____

_____

Step 3: What negative outcomes do you gain by maintaining the current level of anxiety?

_____

_____

_____

Step 4: What is the likely mental, emotional, physical, or spiritual consequences of your current anxiety? List them in each area where applicable*.

Mental	Emotional	Physical	Spiritual
↓	↓	↓	↓

Step 5: Why do you think you are continuing to have patterns of high anxiety and worry that are impacting your choices and decision making?

_____

_____

_____

_____

Step 6: What are the possible outcomes with a change in the actions or behaviors?
- What are the benefits if you are committed to changing your anxiety, actions, behaviors, or thoughts?
- What is the benefit to not changing your anxiety, actions, behaviors, or thoughts?
- What is the benefit of refusing to change your anxiety, actions, behaviors, or thoughts?

Committed to Change	No Change	Refuse to Change
%	%	%

What is the likely percentage of you choosing to change your actions/behaviors and way of thinking? Indicate the numbers in the area above.

Step 7: What is your plan to change? List specific actions and changes. Include details.

_____

_____

_____

_____

_____

_____

_____

This is your *Choice Opportunity* to be   Mentally STRONG™   and less anxious!

Choice Opportunity: Anxiety as a Strength

Expected outcome: Understand the effects of stress and how to use healthy stress to become more productive

Anxiety is a normal emotion to feel during a lifetime. Anxiety should not be prolonged or extreme. Anxiety should not be a persistent state of mind for anyone. This constant state of increased anxiety impacts cognitive functioning, behaviors, choices, and the body's hormonal and chemical balances creating problems and difficulty with attention, focus, and abilities.

When anxiety is periodic, it can be a healthy emotion and promote productivity. At other times, anxiety can be distressing and paralyzing. When anxiety is distressing and paralyzing or continuously at a disproportionately high level, it can be considered a medical condition and appear as nervousness, fear, apprehension, paranoia, and worry.

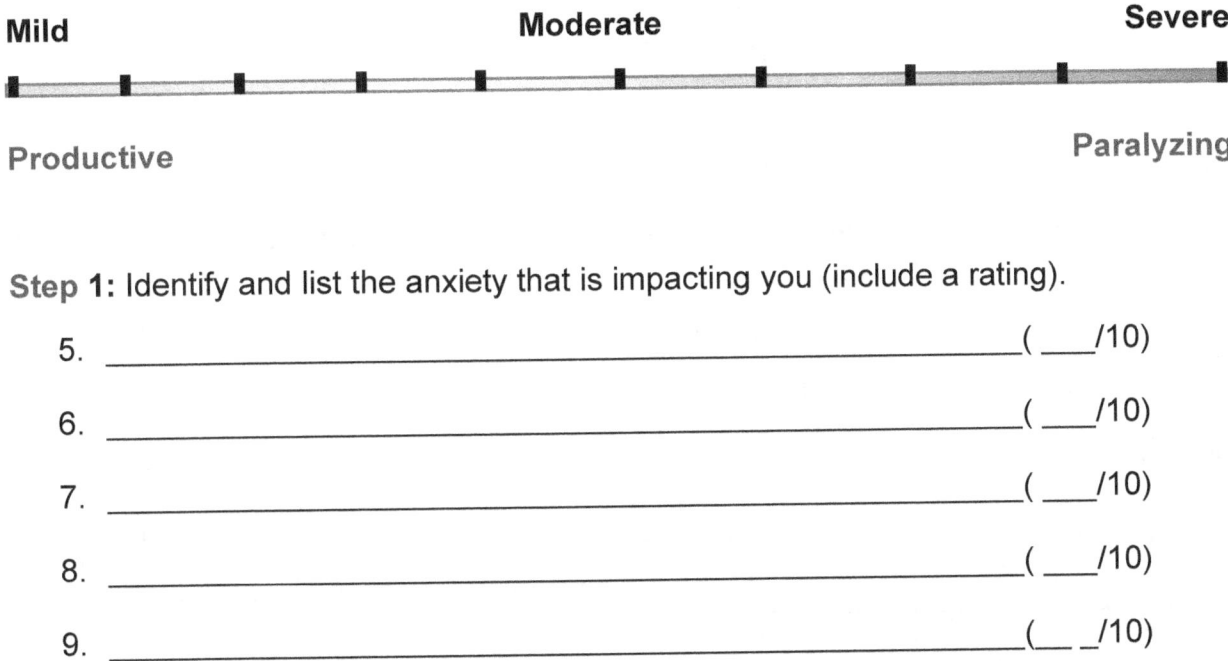

Mild   **Moderate**   **Severe**

Productive   Paralyzing

Step 1: Identify and list the anxiety that is impacting you (include a rating).

5. _____ (___/10)

6. _____ (___/10)

7. _____ (___/10)

8. _____ (___/10)

9. _____ (___ _/10)

Step 2: Create a Personal Vision by reframing the anxiety into a statement of future achievement utilizing anxiety as a source of productivity.

Plan practical coping skills within the actions section to process and manage the anxiety. This should decrease your anxiety levels.

- Grounding
- Thankful thinking

- Gratitude list
- Halting the thoughts with conscious efforts to change.

Personal Vision: Spiritual/Faith, Physical, Mental, Emotional, Financial, Career, Purpose, Relationships, Family, Intelligence, Lifestyle, Sobriety, Other	Actions: Towards Personal Vision	What can I do now? Small steps immediately attainable today	Barriers: What are my obstacles and/or limitations towards my Personal Vision?

Step 3: Review the personal vision you created. Where is your anxiety level now for each of the items listed?

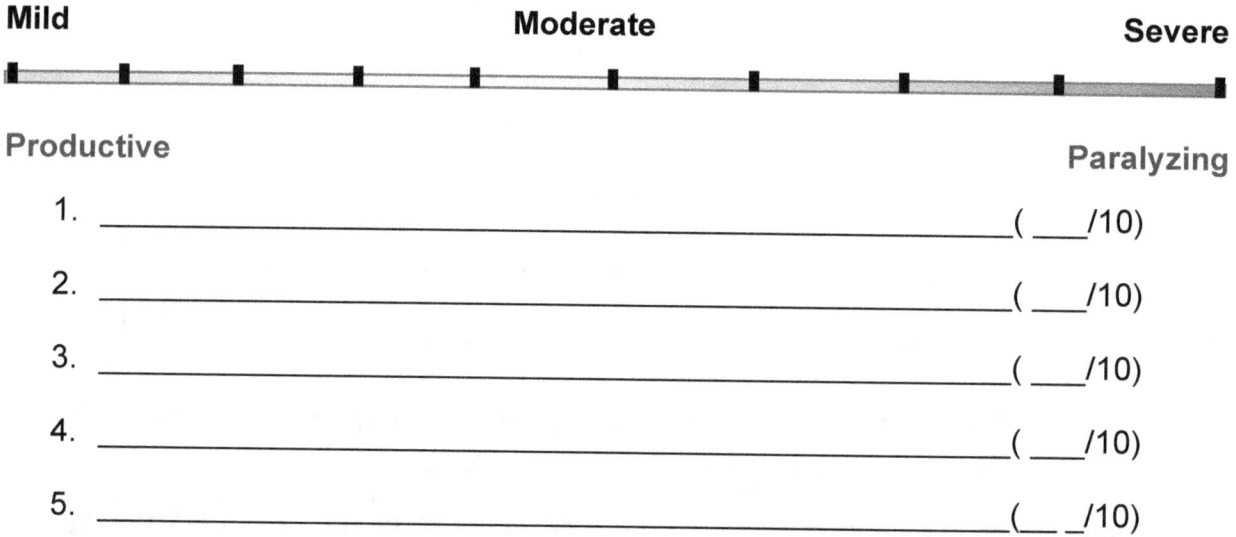

Mild   **Moderate**   **Severe**

Productive   **Paralyzing**

1. _____ (___/10)

2. _____ (___/10)

3. _____ (___/10)

4. _____ (___/10)

5. _____ (___/10)

Step 4: Identify some other things that you can do to reduce your anxiety (into the lower levels where productivity is possible). If there is more you can do, then repeat the Choice Mapping formula and the Personal Vision for more clarity and direction.

This is your *Choice Opportunity* to be Mentally STRONG and use anxiety in a productive way!

Choice Opportunity: Ground then Choose

Expected outcome: Find techniques that will distract your mind, and then challenge yourself to take the next step and make a choice.

"Grounding" is a commonly used term that means gaining control of an unwanted reaction. Grounding is just DISTRACTION. You are using techniques to distract your mind and decrease your reaction to a trigger or other stressor. **We Challenge you to then make a POSITIVE choice in relation to your stressor.**

Step 1: Identify a grounding exercise that you will use the next time that you need to distract your mind. *It could be anything that you think will work for you. You do not need to use the examples below.*

Examples:

- Use a Mantra or repeat a word
- Count Backwards
- Touch Something

- Deep Breathing
- Look at Something
- Focus on a Sound

Describe your grounding technique in detail:

_____

_____

_____

_____

Step 2: What do you need to choose to do?

_____

_____

_____

This is your *Choice Opportunity* to be Mentally STRONG™ and grounded!

Learn more about *The Mentally STRONG Method*: 1-800-55-STRONG ~ www.mentallystrong.com

*The Mentally STRONG Method with Choice Opportunities© Author: Cristi Bundukamara – not for reproduction/distribution

Choice Opportunity: Emotionally Detach

Expected Outcome: Learn how to manage the emotional energy that you are spending.

Identify the person that you wish to detach from emotionally: _____

If you have tried to address a toxic relationship but you cannot cut off the relationship completely, you can make a choice. Do you: (circle one)   ADDRESS IT   LET IT GO

Is this in your best interest?   YES   NO

Identify how much emotional energy you are using trying to fix it, thinking about it, and/or letting it trigger you:

_____

_____

_____

On a scale of 1-10 how much energy have you wasted on this person?

1   2   3   4   5   6   7   8   9   10

Acknowledge the power you have given them:

_____

_____

How have you tried to address this relationship and what was the outcome?

_____

_____

_____

Is there anything else to specifically address?

_____

_____

Accept that you have to let it go and reconsider your definition of "Letting Go."

Letting go is **NOT**:

(Circle what you have wasted time doing)

Accepting

Ignoring

Retaliating

Being Angry

Ruminating

Self-Blame

Allowing Triggers

Feeling Guilty

Letting go **IS**:

Setting Boundaries

Stopping Physical Abuse

Stopping Manipulation

Take Back your power from this person and believe that they can't hurt/trigger you:

_____

_____

_____

_____

_____

This is your *Choice Opportunity* to be   Mentally STRONG™   in detachment.

Learn more about *The Mentally STRONG Method*: **1-800-55-STRONG ~ www.mentallystrong.com**

*The Mentally STRONG Method with Choice Opportunities© Author: Cristi Bundukamara – not for reproduction/distribution

Choice Opportunity: When It's Just Too Much

Expected outcome: Learn to Identify and organize your stress and to prioritize it so it's easier to handle your overwhelming to-do lists or decisions.

Step 1: STOP and BREATHE

Step 2: Give yourself some positive affirmations: _____

_____

_____

"You can do this!"

Step 3: Describe the things that are making you feel like it's all too much (include everything): _____

_____

_____

_____

_____

_____

Step 4: What from the above, if it were by itself, do you feel confident that you could handle?

_____

_____

_____

_____

Step 5: What can you completely let go of? _____

_____

_____

_____

Learn more about *The Mentally STRONG Method*: 1-800-55-STRONG ~ www.mentallystrong.com

*The Mentally STRONG Method with Choice Opportunities© Author: Cristi Bundukamara – not for reproduction/distribution

Step 6: An Organized Brain is a Mentally STRONG Brain! Break down the items into attainable tasks. This is the best way to reduce feelings of overwhelm. Prioritize this list with the easiest items to address first and the most difficult last.

In terms of the "easiest" items, complete and check off as many of these as you can right away.

Some of these items may be more significant or have more weight. They may be time sensitive or have multiple steps. ***Highlight or circle these.*** These items may be toward the bottom of your list, however they will need to be addressed urgently when appropriate.

What I can fix	What I can't fix

This is your *Choice Opportunity* to be Mentally STRONG™ in overwhelm.

Learn more about *The Mentally STRONG Method*: 1-800-55-STRONG ~ www.mentallystrong.com

*The Mentally STRONG Method with Choice Opportunities© Author: Cristi Bundukamara – not for reproduction/distribution

<u>Injustice</u>

"When your world gets turned upside down, choose to land on your feet!" -

Dr. B

You are now ready to complete the next category in Element 3 (Power of Choice). You will now look at your Injustice as identified and filed in Element 2 (Identify and Organize). As you work through this category, consider the following:

- You can overcome the injustices you've experienced with a change in perspective and expectations. Believe in all possibilities and trust yourself to be who you want to be despite others' imposition on your life and dreams.
- Injustices are unfair and difficult to overcome. The underlying issue is that the injustices are not your fault, but you must deal with them and overcome them despite that fact.
- Remind yourself that these social, cultural, societal, political, and other instances of rulemaking are not your problem. They are a weakness or ignorance in the character of the persecutors.

Dr. B's Journey:

Much like the trauma category, I often feel guilty saying that I have experienced injustices (but I have). There are so many injustices in the world around whole people and groups, and many experience horrific trauma based on their race, ethnicity, gender, or sexuality. Again, there is no need to compare myself to them. The point here for me (and for you too) is to identify where injustices have impacted my life, not what my injustices are like in relation to others.

Being an "emotional" woman has led me to feel unfairly judged. I was told that men don't like emotional women and that women are lesser, or not strong, because of their emotions. I was also told that women can't make decisions in stressful situations. These statements are among the many unfair beliefs about women that were taught to me as truths. Comments like these have impacted me for most of my life. I now know that they are not true. Today, I am using my emotions to help others and also hope to change the false beliefs about women and emotions (emotions are not bad).

I am not racist, and didn't grow up in a racist family, so I didn't see racism until I married a Black man and had mixed children. This experience opened up my eyes to the fact that there is systemic racism in the world. I can now see it where I couldn't before. My adopted daughter is afraid while raising her two Black sons. I know how she feels and am similarly worried that my disabled (Black) husband will talk negatively to police. Due to injustices in the world, we both worry that our loved ones could be shot. I don't personally have this same feeling as a White woman and am comfortable when interacting with the police. I now understand the injustices that minorities have to deal with that I don't, and I've had to process those injustices.

To further complicate matters, I have raised two disabled children, and I see how they are treated differently at times. People with disabilities, both physical and mental, have to face similar injustices in the world. As the mother of two disabled children, I've had to process this injustice as well.

Now it's time for you to complete this category (Injustice) for

Identify & Organize	Power of Choice
Core Connections Leave this blank for now, we will come back to it.	Leave this blank for now, we will come back to it.
Triggers • List the triggers in your Thought Map, these are external factors that are causing a reaction.	• Choose what you are going to do with your triggers. Use Choice Opportunities provided.
Grief • List the loss in your Thought Map here	• Use a Choice Opportunity to choose how you are going to work through the grief in your Thought Map.
Trauma • List any trauma from your Thought Map here, you can leave items blank if needed	• Use the provided Choice Opportunities to make choices regarding your trauma.
Negative Thoughts Rating (Belief) • List the negative thought here and rate how much you believe them. ___/10 ___/10 ___/10	• Use the Choice Opportunities provided to help make choices about your negative thoughts.
Behaviors/Choices • Do you have any behaviors or choices in your Thought Map?	• Make choices about your behavior that are in line with your Personal Vision.
Anxiety/Worry Rating (Time Spent) • What worries came up, and rate how much time do you spend? ___/10 ___/10 ___/10	• Use Choice Opportunities to help make choices regarding your anxiety.
Injustices • Write down any injustice that came up in your Thought Map	• What choices can you make about the injustices that have impacted your life?
Spiritual Conflict • Write down any spiritual conflict that came up in your Thought Map	
Addiction • Write down any addiction that may have come up in your Thought Map.	

Repeat this process for each of your identified areas of injustice by completing the Choice Opportunity worksheets attached to this lesson. Give yourself the time needed to fully process each of them. Completing Choice Opportunities for every factor that you identified in element two (Identify and Organize) can increase your insight into how you will move forward in a more positive way towards your personal goals.

Once you have established the Power of Choice in relation to your experiences of injustice, you have once again freed up some of your mental energy and are on your way to taking control of their impact. You can now take the steps towards processing the remaining categories in your metaphorical file cabinet, allowing yourself to continue to understand and work on the central thought identified in the Thought Map.

Can you see why it is helpful to separate injustice from your thoughts and feelings? You can write about it here after you've completed the following Choice Opportunities.

_____

_____

_____

_____

Choice Opportunity: Choose Love

Expected outcome: You will have an opportunity to choose how to react.

An injustice is a situation or influence that you think is unfair or based on judgement of factors or beliefs that are illegal or outdated. Examples could be related to racism, gender, sexuality, political views, personal choices, group dynamics, social status, economic status, mental health status, homelessness, and so much more. You will have an opportunity to embrace the issue and choose how you will react.

Instructions: Answer the questions below to explore the injustice root, effect, and its meaning to you and your personal vision.

Describe the injustice in your Thought Map? _____

_____

_____

Are there examples of how others have reacted in either **love** or **anger** to this injustice?

LOVE   ANGER

Being honest with yourself. If you choose anger, where would that lead and what might be the consequences of your actions?

_____

_____

In what ways could you choose to react in love, and what would the benefit be from that?

Choose to react to your injustice and list your reaction in the following areas. What are you planning to do to overcome the injustice?

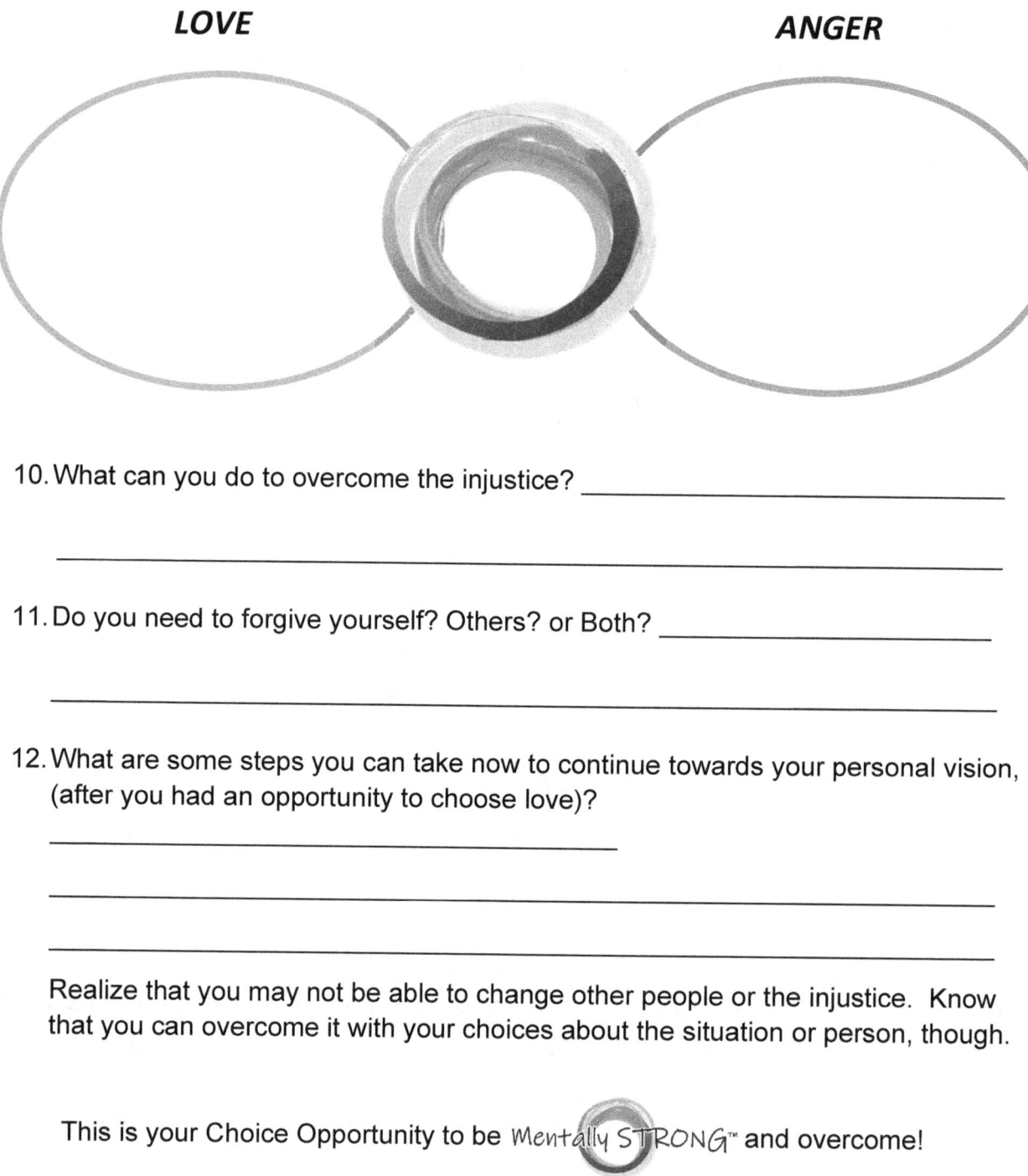

LOVE   *ANGER*

10. What can you do to overcome the injustice? _____

_____

11. Do you need to forgive yourself? Others? or Both? _____

_____

12. What are some steps you can take now to continue towards your personal vision, (after you had an opportunity to choose love)?

_____

_____

_____

Realize that you may not be able to change other people or the injustice. Know that you can overcome it with your choices about the situation or person, though.

This is your Choice Opportunity to be Mentally STRONG™ and overcome!

Learn more about *The Mentally STRONG Method*: 1-800-55-STRONG ~ www.mentallystrong.com

Choice Opportunity: Letter to Offender

Expected Outcome: Opportunity to talk with the person(s) who abused you, took advantage of you, or who hurt you when you were vulnerable.

Instructions: Answer the following questions.

Dear _____,

There was a time when I was vulnerable, and I trusted you to care for me and protect me. Instead, you choose to _____

_____ (What Happened to you).

This impacted me in the past in the following ways: _____

_____

This is still impacting me today in the following ways:

_____

_____

_____

I wish you would have never violated my trust back then. Now, I have more questions. I want to ask you why you chose to do what you did to me.

5. I prayed for you to stop, but you did not. I feel like you have: _____

_____

_____

6. Today, I need to tell you that you impacted me in this way: _____

_____

_____

7. I want you to: _____

_____

8. Today I choose to: _____

_____

_____

9. My steps for this victory will be: _____

_____

This is your *Choice Opportunity* to be   Mentally STRONG™   in my future.

Learn more about *The Mentally STRONG Method*: 1-800-55-STRONG ~ www.mentallystrong.com

Spiritual Conflict

"Spiritual Conflict arises when your thoughts or beliefs about a deity or the universe conflict with your reality or desires." - *Dr. B*

You are now ready to complete the next category in Element 3 (Power of Choice). So, let's keep moving forward. You will now look at your Spiritual Conflict as identified and filed in Element 2 (Identify and Organize). As you work through this category, consider the following:

- Identified spiritual conflict can be many things. Some examples include:
  - God versus religion/church/rules.
  - Blame/anger for bad things happening or not being prevented by God who is so good and kind.
  - Conflict with religious institutions related to social and political issues in the news, such as sexual abuse.
  - Conflict with the foundational rules of the church on social and political topics: sexual abuse, abortion, marriage, sex outside of marriage, gay relationships/marriage, etc.
- Consider this Reflection/Point of View: Go back to who you are in God's eyes and ponder God's plan for your life.
- Your relationship with God is a lifelong journey, just like your journey to be Mentally STRONG. As you make connections and get stronger, God will reveal deeper issues and guide you in developing extraordinary character.

Dr. B's Journey:

I've had an intimate relationship with God since I was 19 years old. My relationship has since grown to become even more individual and personal. When I was young, however, I viewed my relationship with God in terms of very black and white thinking. I believed that just by doing good, I would gain the protection of God. That wasn't the case.

After adopting a three-child sibling group with horrific trauma, I remember telling them that they were now safe. God had brought them to us and we would protect them. That was not true, however. Only a year after their adoption, the oldest sibling died in a drowning accident. Why would God allow this tragedy to happen to a group of innocent children?

I believed that our love (and God's love) would be evident in my adopted children's lives, but honestly, they still struggle with feeling unloved and don't have a strong relationship with God. This has led be to question my own relationship with God at times.

I also believed that through my faith and God's love, my son Reggie would be healed from DRPLA. But when he died in 2016, that created an internal spiritual conflict for me.

This is in a separate category because it is so important to our mental health to work on an individual spiritual relationship (separate from grief). Even after my tragic experiences, I choose to continue to pray and meditate (and to listen for the response). I often feel comforted that my story is not over and that many people will be helped as a result of my suffering. God allowed Reggie to talk to me for just a few seconds and that has eased some of my internal conflict. Although we will not fully understand the spiritual realm here on earth, we can still develop an eternal relationship.

Now it's time for you to complete this category (Spiritual Conflict) for yourself:

Identify & Organize	Power of Choice
Core Connections Leave this blank for now, we will come back to it.	Leave this blank for now, we will come back to it.
Triggers • List the triggers in your Thought Map, these are external factors that are causing a reaction.	• Choose what you are going to do with your triggers. Use Choice Opportunities provided.
Grief • List the loss in your Thought Map here	• Use a Choice Opportunity to choose how you are going to work through the grief in your Thought Map.
Trauma • List any trauma from your Thought Map here, you can leave items blank if needed	• Use the provided Choice Opportunities to make choices regarding your trauma.
Negative Thoughts Rating (Belief) • List the negative thought here and rate how much you believe them. ____/10 ____/10 ____/10	• Use the Choice Opportunities provided to help make choices about your negative thoughts.
Behaviors/Choices • Do you have any behaviors or choices in your Thought Map?	• Make choices about your behavior that are in line with your Personal Vision.
Anxiety/Worry Rating (Time Spent) • What worries came up, and rate how much time do you spend? ____/10 ____/10 ____/10	• Use Choice Opportunities to help make choices regarding your anxiety.
Injustices • Write down any injustice that came up in your Thought Map	• What choices can you make about the injustices that have impacted your life?
Spiritual Conflict • Write down any spiritual conflict that came up in your Thought Map	• Choose what you are going to do with your spiritual conflict.
Addiction • Write down any addiction that may have come up in your Thought Map.	

Repeat this process for each of your identified areas of spiritual conflict by completing the Choice Opportunity worksheets attached to this lesson. Give yourself the time needed to fully process each of them. Completing Choice Opportunities for every factor that you identified in element two (Identify and Organize) can increase your insight into how you will move forward in a more positive way towards your personal goals.

Once you have established the Power of Choice in relation to your spiritual conflict, you have once again freed up some of your mental energy and are on your way to taking control of your spiritual conflict. You can now take the steps towards processing the remaining categories in your metaphorical file cabinet, allowing yourself to continue to understand and work on the central thought identified in the Thought Map.

Can you see why it is helpful to separate spiritual conflict from your thoughts and feelings? You can write about it here after you've completed the following Choice Opportunities.

_____

_____

_____

_____

_____

Choice Opportunity: Why Me?

Expected Outcome: Gain insight into and reframe the "Why me?" question and create a new, more realistic statement.

Step # 1: Think about and describe three logical reasons that "Why me?" is not a fair question:

_____

_____

_____

Step #2 What is your current thought behind the "Why me?" question? Circle all that apply:

Aggravated	Embarrassed	Powerless
Afraid	Empty	Rejected
Alienated	Envious	Sad
Angry	Exhausted	Scared
Annoyed	Fearful	Sensitive
Anxious	Frustrated	Skeptical
Ashamed	Grief	Shocked
Awful	Guilty	Stressed
Chaotic	Heartbroken	Suspicious
Confused	Hurt	Terrified
Crushed	Ignored	Threatened
Depressed	Inadequate	Vulnerable
Devastated	Irritated	Worried
Disappointed	Jealous	Worthless
Drained	Lonely	Withdrawn
Disgusted	Overwhelmed	

Step #3 Make a list of the factors that you CANNOT change:

_____

_____

_____

_____

Step #4 Make a list of the factors that you CAN Change:

_____

_____

_____

_____

Step #5 Write a new, realistic statement that counteracts the question "Why me?":

_____

_____

_____

This is your *Choice Opportunity* to be Mentally STRONG™ and reframe!

Addiction

"Addiction is complex and involves biochemical neurofeedback in the brain. Choose to be stronger than your addiction." - 𝒟𝓇. ℬ

You are now ready to complete the next category in Element 3 (Power of Choice). So, let's keep working on this third element. You will now look at your Addiction as identified and filed in Element 2 (Identify and Organize). As you do so, consider the following:

- Addiction is complex. It is a medical disorder; however, it can also be a choice or a behavior.
- Addiction is not limited to just drugs and alcohol. It can include food, behaviors, excessive spending, sex, gambling, or other actions that negatively impact your life. Risk-taking can also be a form of addiction when done in excess.
- You may need professional help in overcoming the addiction in addition to understanding your behaviors and choices using the Mentally STRONG Method.
- Addiction does not just impact the person addicted; it impacts those who love the person as well.

Dr. B's Journey:

I have a strong family history of addiction (on my biological father's side), and based on the results of psychological testing, I've discovered that I have an addictive personality, too. My experiences substantiate that fact as I used substances as a teen and young adult. I also had an eating disorder and still struggle with an addiction to food.

I was made aware of my predisposition to addiction since childhood. My mom and grandmother used to warn me about it. I believe that the fear of becoming addicted kept me away from using substances for long periods of time, but this fear still impacts me today.

I have also become aware that I have ADD- details are challenging for me. I have tried non-stimulant treatments for my ADD, but they have not been effective. I have been prescribed stimulants for the ADD, but I won't take them for fear of becoming addicted. This decision has been the right decision for me because I understand myself. Similarly, I challenge patients to categorize areas of their life to make better decisions for themselves that are in line with their personal visions.

Professionally, I struggle with writing prescriptions for patients because of my own personal fear of addiction (even if I know that the medicine will help them). My experience with addiction causes my hesitation in those cases, but I have learned to separate myself (and my fears) from those choices.

Now it's time for you to complete this category (Addiction) for yourself:

Identify & Organize	Power of Choice
Core Connections Leave this blank for now, we will come back to it.	Leave this blank for now, we will come back to it.
Triggers • List the triggers in your Thought Map, these are external factors that are causing a reaction.	• Choose what you are going to do with your triggers. Use Choice Opportunities provided.
Grief • List the loss in your Thought Map here	• Use a Choice Opportunity to choose how you are going to work through the grief in your Thought Map.
Trauma • List any trauma from your Thought Map here, you can leave items blank if needed	• Use the provided Choice Opportunities to make choices regarding your trauma.
Negative Thoughts Rating (Belief) • List the negative thought here and rate how much you believe them. ____/10 ____/10 ____/10	• Use the Choice Opportunities provided to help make choices about your negative thoughts.
Behaviors/Choices • Do you have any behaviors or choices in your Thought Map?	• Make choices about your behavior that are in line with your Personal Vision.
Anxiety/Worry Rating (Time Spent) • What worries came up, and rate how much time do you spend? ____/10 ____/10 ____/10	• Use Choice Opportunities to help make choices regarding your anxiety.
Injustices • Write down any injustice that came up in your Thought Map	• What choices can you make about the injustices that have impacted your life?
Spiritual Conflict • Write down any spiritual conflict that came up in your Thought Map	• Choose what you are going to do with your spiritual conflict.
Addiction • Write down any addiction that may have come up in your Thought Map.	• Make choices around the addiction in your life.

Repeat this process for each of your identified areas of addiction by completing the Choice Opportunity worksheets attached to this lesson. Give yourself the time needed to fully process each of them. Completing Choice Opportunities for every factor that you identified in element two (Identify and Organize) can increase your insight into how you will move forward in a more positive way towards your personal goals.

Once you have established the Power of Choice in relation to your addiction, you have once again freed up some of your mental energy and are on your way to taking control of your addiction. You can now take the final step towards processing the remaining category in your metaphorical file cabinet, allowing yourself to continue to understand and work on the central thought identified in the Thought Map.

Choice Opportunity: Benefit Analysis - Addiction

Expected Outcome: Self-analysis of your thoughts, the situation, and consideration of the options available to take positive actions in relation to your addiction.

The purpose of a benefit analysis is to consider all of the factors in a situation and to decide based on the facts disclosed during the investigation (of the factors for the relevant components impacting the situation). When you have areas of your behavior or personality that are maladaptive and not supporting your personal vision, it is important to figure out why you continue to do the same things repeatedly expecting a different outcome. If you can understand the motivation, even subconsciously, you can make a more conscious effort to change your behaviors with different choices.

Step 1: Identify the addictions from your Mentally STRONG Method session. Write them here and take time to reflect on where you are now with your addiction(s).

_____.

_____.

Step 2: Is this where you want to be?   Yes / No

Step 3: What benefit do you gain by maintaining the current addictions?

_____

_____

Step 4: What negative outcomes do you gain by maintaining the current addictions?

_____

_____

Step 5: What is the likely mental, emotional, physical, or spiritual consequences of your addictions? List them in each area where applicable*.

Mental   Emotional   Physical   Spiritual

Step 5: Why do you think you are continuing to have the addictions? Identify any behavior reinforcers in your current situation.

_____

_____

_____

_____

Step 6: What are the possible outcomes with a change in the actions or behaviors?
- What are the benefits if you are committed to changing your addiction, actions, behaviors, or thoughts?
- What is the benefit to not changing your addiction, actions, behaviors, or thoughts?
- What is the benefit of refusing to change your addiction, actions, behaviors, or thoughts?

Committed to Change	No Change	Refuse to Change
%	%	%

What is the likely percentage of you choosing to change your actions/behaviors and way of thinking? Indicate the numbers in the area above.

Step 7: What is your plan to change? List specific actions and changes and include details.

_____

_____

_____

_____

_____

_____

This is YOUR choice opportunity to be Mentally STRONG™ with your story

Learn more about *The Mentally STRONG Method*: **1-800-55-STRONG ~ www.mentallystrong.com**

Choice Opportunity: Take Responsibility in Addiction

Expected outcome: Acknowledge responsibility in your addiction.

Personal Choice:
You can
overcome
addiction.

Do the biology
of Addiction
Choice
Opportunity

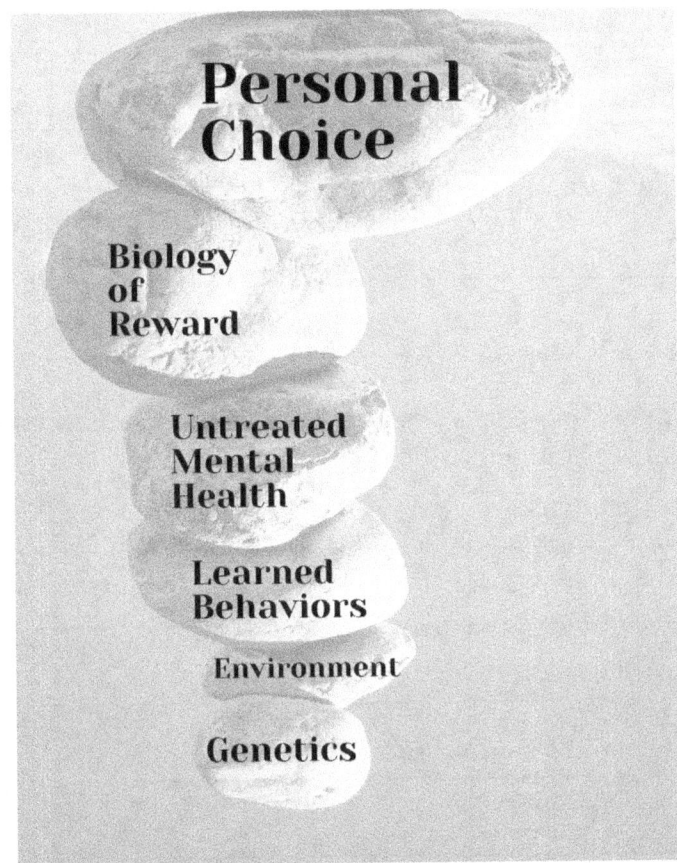

If needed: Seek
appropriate medical
attention.

Struggle with depression,
anxiety, mania, psychosis,
overwhelming emotions?

Addiction became your
coping mechanism.

External factors leading
to addictions.

Genetic predisposition.

Personal Choice: Today we challenge you to choose to overcome your addiction.
Your choices:

_____

_____

Biology of Reward: Request and complete the Choice Opportunity: Biology of Addiction
and consider the use of medication assistance treatment.

Untreated Mental Health: Do you struggle with depression, anxiety, psychosis,
overwhelming emptions?   Yes   No
If yes, then begin to develop a plan to treat your mental health concerns.

_____

_____

Learn more about *The Mentally STRONG Method*: 1-800-55-STRONG ~ www.mentallystrong.com

Learned Behaviors: Identify if you had a role model for addiction in your life?

_____

_____

Identify other areas where you learned addictive behaviors:

_____

_____

Environment: Identify experiences, triggers, relationships, situation, and communities that have contributed to your addiction:

Experiences: _____

Triggers: _____

Relationships: _____

Situations: _____

Communities: _____

Genetics: Genetic predisposition is only a small influence on your addiction. The Power of Choice is stronger than your genetics.

List the positive choices you need to make to be successful._____

_____

_____

_____

_____

This is your _Choice Opportunity_ to be   Mentally STRONG   and make positive choices.

Choice Opportunity: Who am I Without Addiction

Expected outcome: Envision your life without addiction and what that would look like.

Instructions: Answer the following questions.

Addiction has changed your life, most likely through negative changes.

1. Identify how addiction has changed your life.
   a. Family Relationships? _____
   b. Work/Employment? _____
   c. Friends/Social? _____
   d. Character? _____
   e. Things you enjoy doing? _____
   f. Beliefs/Morals/Ethics? _____
   g. Driving? _____
   h. Housing? _____
   i. Financial? _____
   j. Physical Health? _____
   k. Mental Health? _____

2. List 10 positive attributes or qualities about yourself:
   a. _____ f. _____
   b. _____ g. _____
   c. _____ h. _____
   d. _____ i. _____
   e. _____ j. _____

3. List how you will choose to positively change your life as you overcome your addictions to work on your personal vision?
   a. _____
   b. _____
   c. _____
   d. _____
   e. _____

4. How will you choose to align your positive qualities and character attributes with your behavior and choices to support your personal vision? _____

_____

_____

5. How will these changes impact these areas of your life?

Mental	Emotional	Physical	Spiritual
↓	↓	↓	↓

6. How will these changes impact these other areas of your life?

Family	Employment	Social/Friends	Choices

7. How will these changes impact these additional areas of your life?

Housing	Driving	Education	_____

This is your Choice Opportunity to be 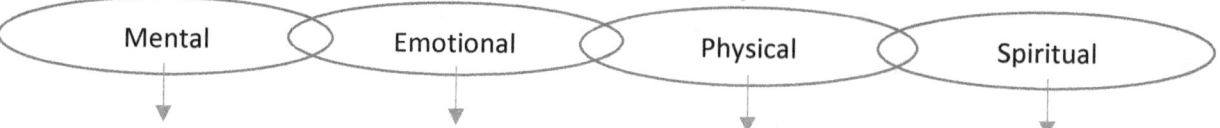 Mentally STRONG™ with making your future positive!

Core Connections

"You ARE Mentally STRONG!" - 𝒟𝓇. ℬ

You are now ready to complete this category in Element 3 (Power of Choice). Go you! So, let's finalize this third element by taking this step. This is the one that we said we would come back to.

As part of this step, you can now refer back to the blank area on your Identify and Organize (Element 2) sheet that we have not addressed yet: "Core Connections." This is the most important category, and many times, you need to have created and organized several Thought Maps before you start to discover your own Core Connections. That's the reason this is the final step in Element 3. When you are completing this step, consider the following:

- A Core Connection is a theme in your life that causes some reaction for you. Take a step back and look at the big picture of your Thought Map. This will enable you to identify your Core Connections and list them here. They can consist of:
    - Themes involving choices/behaviors. These identified themes, connections, and links will be useful in understanding the other elements.
    - Past and current Core Connections with actions/inaction and patterns in your ways of thinking.
    - Influences in choices or decision-making that may be maladaptive, but protective.
    - Contributing factors which may not have been dealt/processed that are impacting your current thinking and behaviors.

Dr. B's Journey:

I added the Core Connections category after using the Mentally STRONG Method on my patients because I noticed that they were having a hard time identifying the patterns and connections that have been impacting them since childhood. Core Connections are different from negative thoughts because negative thoughts can be reframed and minimized with positive thinking (Core Connections cannot). You can often identify when a negative thought started, for example, the negative thought that I am fat began when my uncle called me fat when I was nine.

Core Connections, on the other hand, are more of an ingrained belief system that has been negatively impacting a person for a long period of time (and will likely remain present throughout their life). I've believed that I am not good enough for as long as I can remember, and that belief still impacts me today. Telling myself that I'm not good enough is my strongest, and most deeply embedded, Core Connection. This deep core connection can manifest in many ways; I tell myself that I'm not pretty enough, I'm not perfect enough, I'm not skinny enough or that I don't have enough energy or motivation.

Although you do have to use positive thinking to counter your Core Connections, they are harder to eradicate and will likely come up often throughout your Mentally Strong journey. It's the same for me.

Now it's your turn to complete this category (Core Connections) for yourself:

Identify & Organize	Power of Choice
Core Connections • List your Core Connections here.	• Make choices regarding your Core Connections.
Triggers • List the triggers in your Thought Map, these are external factors that are causing a reaction.	• Choose what you are going to do with your triggers. Use Choice Opportunities provided.
Grief • List the loss in your Thought Map here	• Use a Choice Opportunity to choose how you are going to work through the grief in your Thought Map.
Trauma • List any trauma from your Thought Map here, you can leave items blank if needed	• Use the provided Choice Opportunities to make choices regarding your trauma.

Negative Thoughts   Rating (Belief)
• List the negative thought here and rate how much you believe them.   ____/10
   ____/10
   ____/10
	• Use the Choice Opportunities provided to help make choices about your negative thoughts.

Behaviors/Choices • Do you have any behaviors or choices in your Thought Map?	• Make choices about your behavior that are in line with your Personal Vision.

Anxiety/Worry   Rating (Time Spent)
• What worries came up, and rate how much time do you spend? ____/10
  ____/10
  ____/10
	• Use Choice Opportunities to help make choices regarding your anxiety.

Injustices • Write down any injustice that came up in your Thought Map	• What choices can you make about the injustices that have impacted your life?
Spiritual Conflict • Write down any spiritual conflict that came up in your Thought Map	• Choose what you are going to do with your spiritual conflict.
Addiction Write down any addiction that may have come up in your Thought Map.	• Make choices around the addiction in your life.

Author: Cristi Bundukamara

Repeat this process for each of your identified Core Connections by completing the Choice Opportunity worksheets attached to this lesson. Give yourself the time needed to fully process each of them. Completing Choice Opportunities for your Core Connections can increase your insight into how you will move forward in a more positive way towards reaching your personal goals.

Once you have established the Power of Choice in relation to your Core Connections, you have once again freed up your mental energy and are on your way towards understanding how these Core Connections influence you.

Choice Opportunity: Core Connections

Expected Outcome: Learn what core connections are and how to recognize them in yourself.

Definition: Core Connections are themes in your life that cause some reaction.

Step 1: Thought Map

Before moving forward with this Choice Opportunity, go through the thought mapping process. You may use a Thought Map that you previously completed.

Step 2: Find Your Core Connections

What was the central thought in your Thought Map? _____

Describe your history of having this same reaction? _____

_____

_____

Dig Deeper, what hurts? _____

_____

Step 3: Be Aware

Trigger → REACTION → Core Connection

Just being aware of your Core Connections can decrease and reduce the intensity of your reaction to a trigger.

This is your *Choice Opportunity* to be Mentally STRONG™ with insight!

Learn more about *The Mentally STRONG Method*: 1-800-55-STRONG ~ www.mentallystrong.com

Congratulations. You've completed the third element of this process but will continue to refer back to it as it's ongoing. Next you will see an example of my Power of Choice. I hope that it provides context around the work that you (and I) have been doing.

Identify & Organize	Power of Choice
The Mentally STRONG Method: Element 2	The Mentally STRONG Method: Element 3
Core Connections • NOT Good enough •	I am doing my best
Triggers • Wrong decision • insinuate I'm not smart. • Weight gain	No one is Perfect I am smarter than I give myself credit for
Grief • Reggie 17yo son died. DRPLA. • Johnny 13yo died drowning • Antisiptory grief Miah.	I take time at least a couple times a year for controlled grief.
Trauma • Date Rape • Physical/Emotional Abuse •	I choose aknowhedge it's impact, chose strength.
Negative Thoughts Rating (Belief) • not Smart 3 /10 • Fat 4 /10 • ____ /10	I am above auerage I am not Fat
Behaviors/Choices • impulsive • •	Choose self Control and forgiveness
Anxiety/Worry Rating (Time Spent) • Wrong decisions. 4 /10 • ____ /10 • ____ /10	No one is perfect but I'm doing my best
Injustices • NOT Fair amount hardship • NOT Fair ultra rare no treatment • African Spouce + children	I choose never give up I choose find Joy

Spiritual Conflict
• Trusting God's Voice
     Protection
     love
•
	I choose continue
	working on my relationship
	pray and listen

Addiction • Fear getting addicted. •	I choose to Control urges to not care.

Section 6

Element 4: Personal Vision

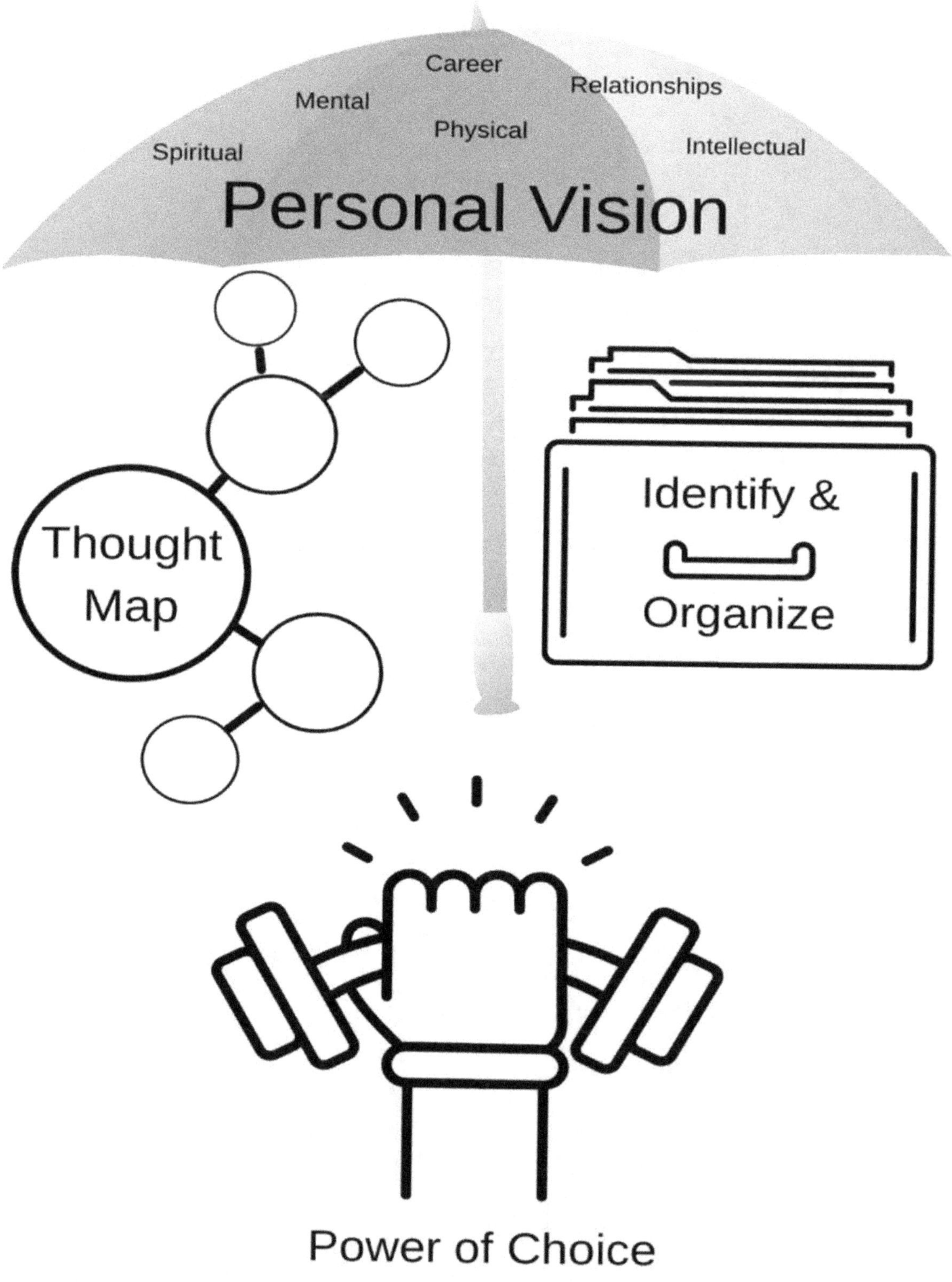

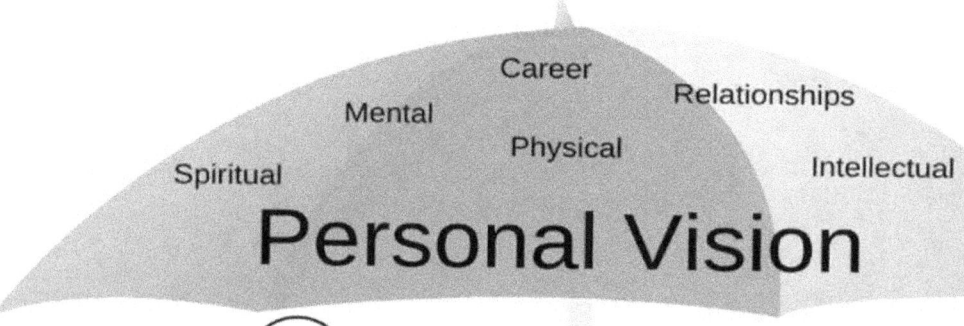

Spiritual   Mental   Career   Physical   Relationships   Intellectual

Personal Vision

Thought Map

Identify & Organize

Power of Choice

Personal Vision

"You have to believe and take action to achieve your visions." - *Dr. B*

You are now ready to tackle Element 4 (creating your Personal Vision). This is the final element in the Mentally Strong Method. You are making some serious progress. In this element, you will be challenged to make choices and move towards change. Remember that regardless of your internal and external influences, you always have a choice- that includes the choice to be happy.

Because you are your own unique person, you can have multiple Personal Visions in various areas of your life (different from those of others). Over time, your Personal Visions will evolve as you make more and more progress towards mental strength. You will complete some visions with a natural conclusion, and then form and move on to others.

Understand that creating a Personal Vision is all about you. It can encompass all of your dreams, goals, and aspirations. When you work on your Personal Vision, think about what you truly want deep down inside. Aim high, dream big, and do not limit yourself. If you could make anything happen for yourself, what would it be? This is where you should be setting your sights (you can do it).

Be aware that your Personal Visions are not set in stone either. You can always evaluate and adjust them later on if needed. In the first three elements, you recognized the past, acknowledged your thoughts and behaviors, and then organized and made sense of them. Now, in this final element, you will choose to act in line with your Personal Vision(s). This element can help you change the future into what you want for yourself, and I know that you want more.

When working on your Personal Vision, here are some Important Points to Consider:

- Creating a Personal Vision is an activity that focuses on your future. In order to have the best outcome, you will need to use positive and uplifting thinking. Your Personal Vision is about what you want for your future; it is not about fixing your past experiences.
- The purpose of the Personal Vision element (within this process) is to take the insight obtained while completing the other elements and use it to create a Personal Vision for the best version of yourself.
- Your Personal Visions will evolve with time as you change and grow Mentally STRONG.
- Some of your Personal Visions will ebb and flow as you move through a stage in your life, and that's good.

As you set your Personal Vision, beware of possible roadblocks and use sound strategies to move forward. Keep in mind the following:

- When working on your Personal Vision, avoid focusing your attention on previous experiences or past choices. If you find yourself fixating on the past, then re-work the Mentally STRONG Method before you proceed to this fourth element.
- You should also avoid talking negatively about yourself or your future. Remember that your Personal Vision involves the best possible version of yourself (you can get there). You have the control. Avoid letting the fear of change, or the fear of your own potential, influence you. If you are experiencing either of those fears, then go back and complete a Mentally STRONG Method session about it before you move forward.

Are you ready to create your Personal Vision using the instructions for Element 4 of the Mentally STRONG Method?

I hope so. Before you begin, however, understand that honing your Personal Vision is a lifelong practice which draws on your mental strength, and is one in which you will continue to create and maintain your Personal Visions.

Some of these visions may conclude and others may need to be halted. Still others may require changes in order to adapt to your life/personal situations. Remind yourself that you are not limited in the number of your Personal Visions either. You can create a Personal Vision in many different areas of your life (and I encourage you to do so).

Further, the timeframe of your Personal Vision is variable and determined entirely by you. You are in control of when you will accomplish your Personal Vision. Realize that some Personal Visions will have a natural conclusion with the completion of a task, job, or event. For other Personal Visions, there will be no time limit and the Personal Vision will morph as you change.

A Personal Vision can be applied to many different areas of your life, but the following are examples of where you can create and evolve with your Personal Visions:

- Spiritual/Faith
- Physical
- Mental
- Emotional
- Financial
- Career/Professional
- Purpose

- Relationships
- Family
- Intelligence/Education
- Lifestyle
- Self-Control
- Other areas of importance to you

So, you've done the work in the previous three elements. Now, let's take the first of four steps towards completing Element 4 and creating your Personal Vision:

Personal Vision

In this first step, you will construct Personal Visions for different areas of your life. Keep in mind that:

- The Personal Visions you develop should be as clear as possible for your future. Be sure to include a lot of details and specific information. In crafting your Personal Vision, it's best to understand what you are striving for within that vision. Do some brainstorming here and really dig deep to uncover what that is.
- You have come too far to avoid your full potential at this point in the Mentally STRONG Method, so don't hold back with your dreams, desires, and goals (you can get there).
- Your Personal Vision should be attainable. So, although I encourage you to dream big, temper it with a healthy dose of realism.
- Be flexible with your time frame.

- You can have more than one Personal Vision in any area so don't limit yourself.
- The creation of your Personal Vision does not have any rules (you're in charge). You are the architect with the creative license to make it your own so run with it.

Now take the time to develop your own meaningful Personal Visions related to multiple areas of your life using the provided worksheet. They will be different for everyone as we are all diverse and special with our own unique goals.

The Mentally STRONG Method
Personal Vision

Personal Vision: Spiritual/Faith, Physical, Mental, Emotional, Financial, Career, Purpose, Relationships, Family, Intelligence, Lifestyle, Sobriety, Other	Write down your Personal Visions in the top row for any number of areas, there are some suggestions listed here.	I encourage you to create a Personal Vision in more than one area.	
Actions: Towards Personal Vision			
What can I do now: Small steps immediately attainable today			
BARRIERS: What are my obstacles and/or limitations towards my Personal Vision?			

Actions

Now that you have finished creating your Personal Vision you are ready to move on to the second step which involves developing actions.

Develop Specific Actions to Achieve Your Personal Vision.

When working on this step, consider the following:

- Actions are things that you must do (or need to complete) to achieve your Personal Vision.
- Completing your actions is like going up stairs. In order to get to the top, you must walk up the stairs step by step. To achieve your Personal Vision, you must similarly approach it one step at a time. So:
  - Be specific on the actions that you need to take in order to achieve your Personal Vision.
  - Remember that a vision without a plan is just a dream. Although it is often helpful to dream, you must believe in your dream and take action to achieve it.
  - Remind yourself to make time in your day to take those actions.
  - Work to develop the mental strength to slowly make progress towards your Personal Visions.
  - Keep in mind that some actions may not be specific if the actions are out of your control.
  - Sometimes doing nothing right now is your course of action and will be necessary. The ability to be able to do nothing may take some patience, and that's okay.

Now it's time for you to take this second step by completing the Actions section on the provided worksheet:

The Mentally STRONG Method
Personal Vision

Personal Vision: Spiritual/Faith, Physical, Mental, Emotional, Financial, Career, Purpose, Relationships, Family, Intelligence, Lifestyle, Sobriety, Other	Write down your Personal Visions in the top row for any number of areas, there are some suggestions listed here.	I encourage you to create a Personal Vision in more than one area.	
Actions: Towards Personal Vision	In this row, list out all the actions you can think of that you will need to do to move closer to your Personal Vision.		
What can I do now: Small steps immediately attainable today			
BARRIERS: What are my obstacles and/or limitations towards my Personal Vision?			

Never Give Up!

<u>Now</u>

It looks like you are now ready for the next step in this fourth element (Personal Vision). This is where you look at what you can do right now.

In this step, ask yourself, what small steps can I take now?

- Identify tangible tasks when there is something to be done today.
- Know that sometimes the answer is that nothing can be done today.
- Understand that sometimes the answer is to just patiently wait.
- Remember that sometimes the answer is to pray about the situation.
- Remind yourself that most times there is something you can do NOW to reach your Personal Vision.
- Keep in mind that these actions are specific and immediately attainable tasks that are in line with your Personal Vision.

Now you will use the provided worksheet to complete the areas related to Step 3: (Now):

The Mentally STRONG Method
Personal Vision

Personal Vision: Spiritual/Faith, Physical, Mental, Emotional, Financial, Career, Purpose, Relationships, Family, Intelligence, Lifestyle, Sobriety, Other	Write down your Personal Visions in the top row for any number of areas, there are some suggestions listed here.	I encourage you to create a Personal Vision in more than one area.	
Actions: Towards Personal Vision	In this row, list out all the actions you can think of that you will need to do to move closer to your Personal Vision.		
What can I do now: Small steps immediately attainable today	In this row, list out what you can do today to move closer to your Personal Vision.		
BARRIERS: What are my obstacles and/or limitations towards my Personal Vision?			

Never Give Up!

Barriers

You are moving right along. Now it's time to progress to the fourth and final step in Element 4 (Personal Vision). This is the step where you consider your barriers.

As part of this step, you must acknowledge obstacles or limitations related to your Personal Vision. Keep in mind the following:

- Barriers are defined as circumstances, obstacles, or situations that keep you from attaining your Personal Vision and making progress.
- These barriers may be internal and related to thoughts and feelings.
- Ask yourself the following questions:
  - What are your identified barriers?
  - What responsibilities may get in the way of your achieving your Personal Visions?
  - What worries are interfering with your Personal Visions?
  - Are there any natural barriers which cannot be changed or overcome? Realize that this is a possibility.
- This step might require you to alter and adapt your Personal Vision to make it achievable for you. As such:
  - Form a plan to challenge the identified barriers that can be overcome.
  - Know that you may need to complete a Mentally STRONG Method session to map out the barriers identified in order to formulate a better understanding and strategy to adapt so do so if needed.

Now it's time for you to complete this fourth step by filling out the area on the provided worksheet related to Barriers:

The Mentally STRONG Method
Personal Vision

Personal Vision: Spiritual/Faith, Physical, Mental, Emotional, Financial, Career, Purpose, Relationships, Family, Intelligence, Lifestyle, Sobriety, Other	Write down your Personal Visions in the top row for any number of areas, there are some suggestions listed here.	I encourage you to create a Personal Vision in more than one area, repeat these steps for each one.	
Actions: Towards Personal Vision	In this row, list out all the actions you can think of that you will need to do to move closer to your Personal Vision.		
What can I do now: Small steps immediately attainable today	In this row, list out what you can do today to move closer to your Personal Vision.		
BARRIERS: What are my obstacles and/or limitations towards my Personal Vision?	In this row, list any barriers that may be a challenge in reaching your Personal Vision		

Never Give Up!

Dr. B's Journey: Personal Vision

One of my Personal Visions is to provide exceptional loving care to my husband and daughter with DRPLA. Actions I can take are to manage anticipatory grief, and make sure to set up plenty of resources. Right now, I can enjoy what they can do today. The barrier to this vision is that it is emotionally difficult.

Another one of my Personal Visions is to have an authentic, individual, personal relationship with God, that sparks curiosity in others and never appears judgmental. An action I can take towards this vision is to continue to seek and listen. Right now, I can practice living in the present, and barriers include hardships, especially losing Reggie, and likely losing my husband and daughter.

A third Personal Vision of mine is to empower millions of people to see their worth and find purpose and mental strength. Actions I can take are to continue to share the Mentally STRONG Method and continue to grow the business. Right now, I can continue to be genuine in helping others. One barrier for this vision is the dependent culture that we live in.

The Mentally STRONG Method
Personal Vision

Personal Vision: Spiritual/Faith, Physical, Mental, Emotional, Financial, Career, Purpose, Relationships, Family, Intelligence, Lifestyle, Sobriety, Other	Provide exceptional loving care to my husband and daughter with DRPLA	Have an authentic individual, personal relationship with God, that sparks curiosity in others and never appears judgemental	Empower millions of people to see their worth, find purpose + mental strength
Actions: Towards Personal Vision	manage anticipitary grief. make sure plenty resources	Continue to work through spiritual conflict help others	Share Mentally STRONG method grow business help others
What can I do now: Small steps immediately attainable today	Enjoy what they can do today	Live in present Seek + listen	work hard every day with motivation to help others
BARRIERS: What are my obstacles and/or limitations towards my Personal Vision?	No Treatment no Cure likely death emotionally draining	Hardships expecially losing Reggie, likly losing husband and daughter	Dependent Culture

Never Give Up!

209

<u>Activity Time!</u>

Complete the following Choice Opportunity, "Who am I" to help reinforce your Personal Vision. Use this exercise to explore how you define yourself. Doing so may give you a jumping off point on how to create your own Personal Visions.

Choice Opportunity: Who Am I?

Expected outcome: Gain knowledge and insight into your purpose and in an attempt to define yourself.

Knowing who you are, what you want, and where you want to go is crucial towards fulfilling your purpose in your life. The following questions can help you discover who you are, what you want, and where you want to go.

1. I like myself because:

_____

_____

2. I feel good about:

_____

_____

3. My friends would say that I have a great:

_____

_____

4. I am loved by:

_____

_____

5. People say I am good at:

_____

_____

6. Five positive things others say about me:

_____

_____

7. I consider myself a good:

_____

_____

8. I have overcome:

_____

_____

9. I enjoy doing:

_____

_____

10. I know that I will attain my personal vision, because I am:

_____

_____

11. People compliment me about:

_____

_____

12. I feel good when:

_____

_____

13. I've been successful at:

_____

_____

14. I laugh when I think about:

_____

_____

15. The traits I admire about myself are:

_____

_____

16. I think positively about myself when:

_____

_____

Congratulations! You've made it through the 4th (and final) Element in the Mentally Strong Method. Go You! You now have the tools and the process you need to become (and stay) Mentally Strong. Remember that this is a lifelong process so you will keep repeating it (I do), but as you do, you will watch your Personal Visions come to fruition as you become armed with the power to think, organize, and choose.

Now that, you've finished this final element, complete the Mentally Strong Scale again to check back in with yourself in terms of your progress.

Mentally STRONG Scale

How confident are you that you can think through your problems/issues, organize your thoughts, and make decisions that you are proud of?

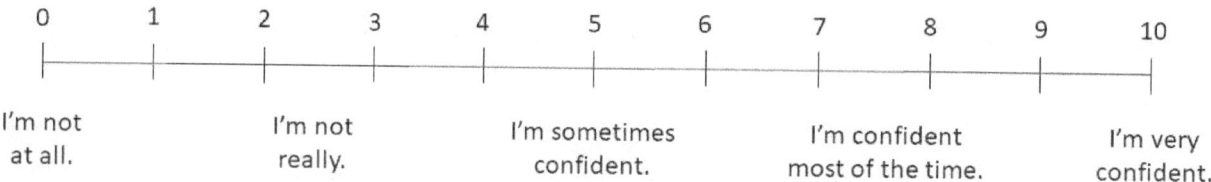

How confident are you that you have insight into your past and how it impacts your thoughts and mood today?

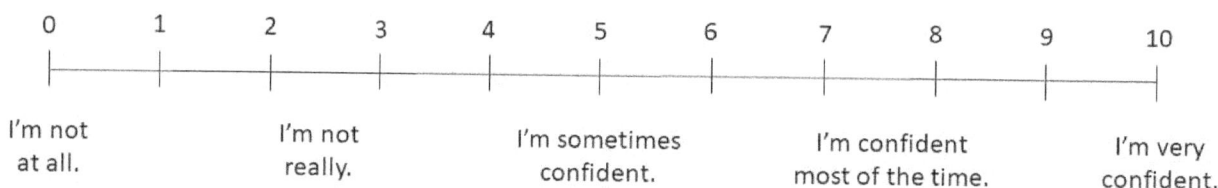

How confident are you that you can manage your triggers so that they don't impact your thoughts and/or mood?

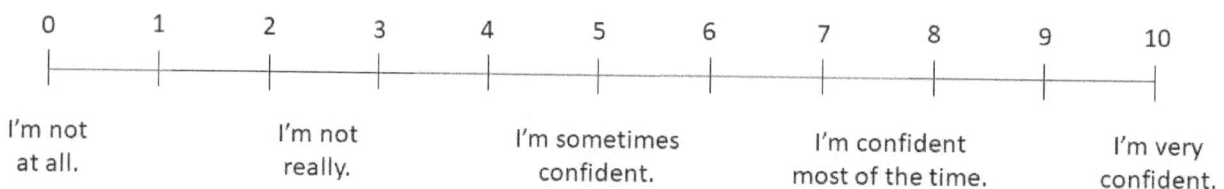

How confident are you that you have processed grief in your life?

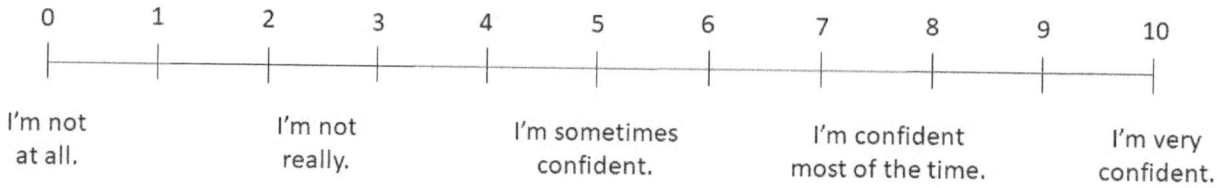

How confident are you that you have processed your trauma and can manage the impact trauma has had on your life? If you have never experienced trauma, circle 10. This is a protective factor that you can be grateful for.

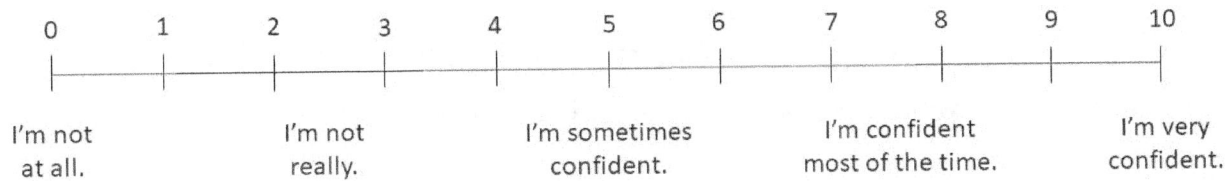

How confident are you that you can consistently reframe your negative thoughts into realistic positive thoughts?

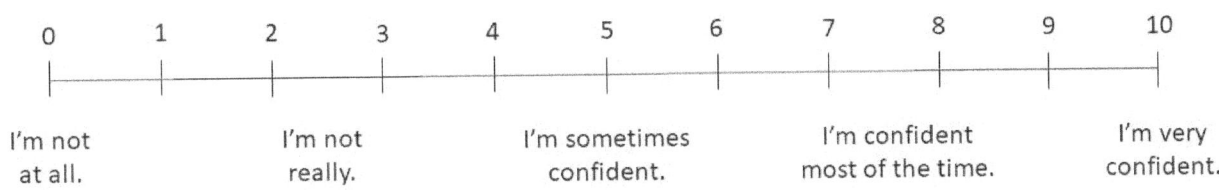

How confident are you that you have insight into how past decisions are currently impacting your thoughts, mood, and life?

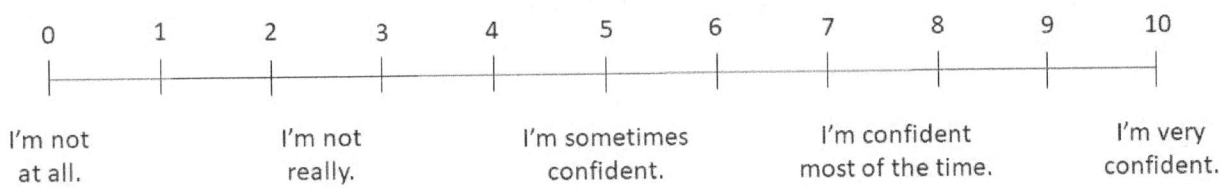

How confident are you in your ability to change behaviors that have a negative impact on you?

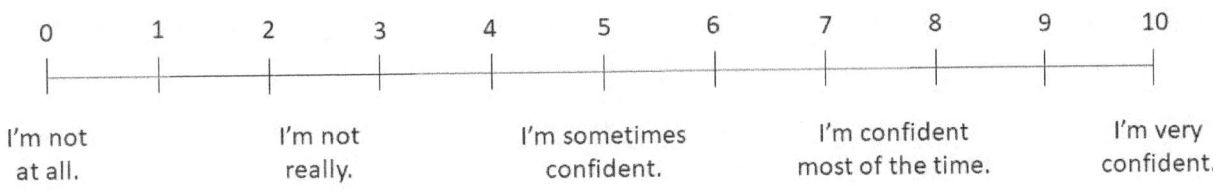

Are you confident in your ability to manage your anxiety, worry or fear?

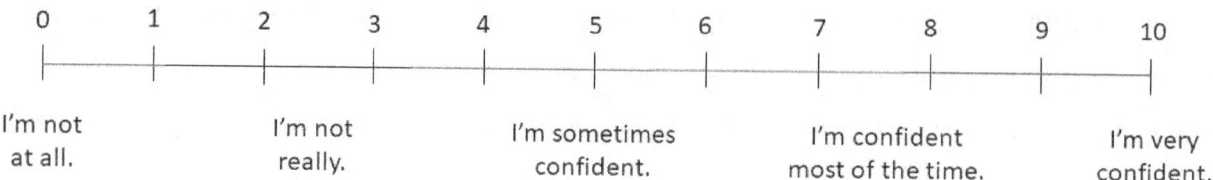

How confident are you that you can think, organize those thoughts, and choose a productive response when you experience or witness an injustice?

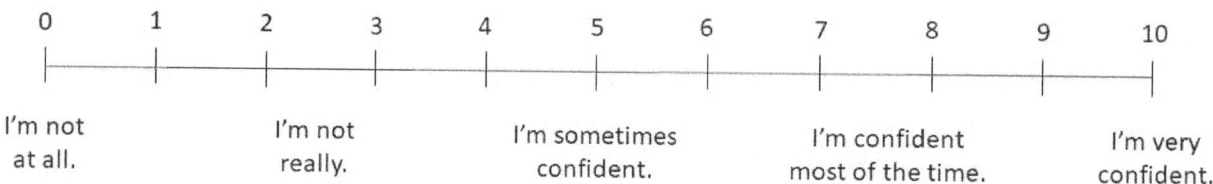

How confident are you in managing how injustices impact your thoughts and mood?

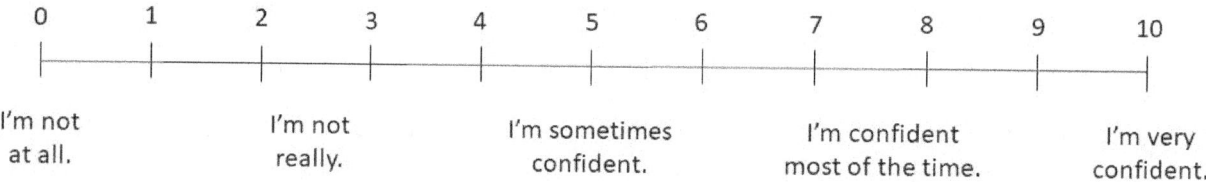

How confident are you in your spiritual relationship or belief system that improves your quality of life?

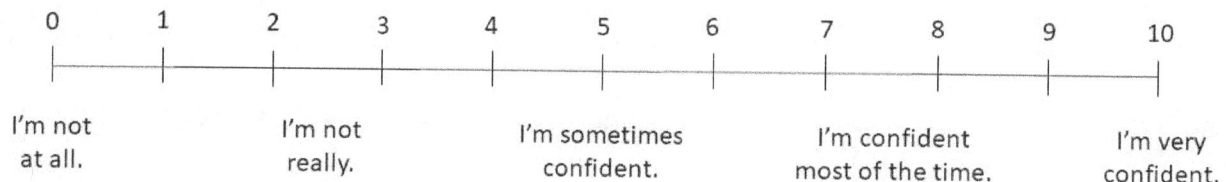

How confident are you that you can manage your addiction? If you have never experienced addiction, circle 10. This is a protective factor that you can be grateful for.

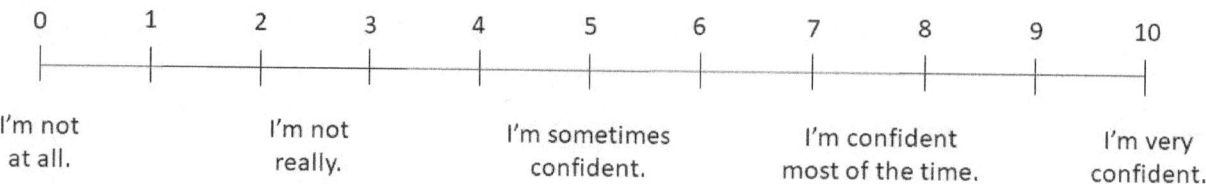

How confident are you in your ability to make healthy choices in line with what you want in your life?

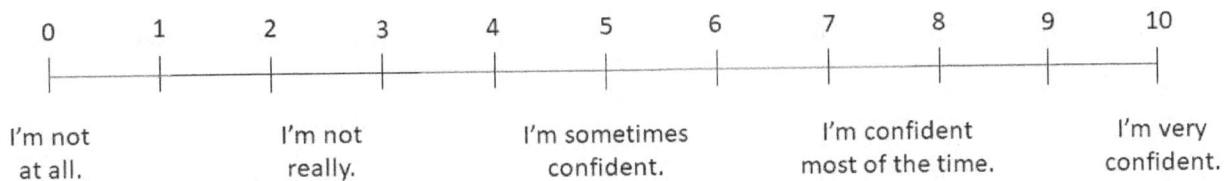

How confident are you in your ability to make meaningful choices in line with what you want in your relationships?

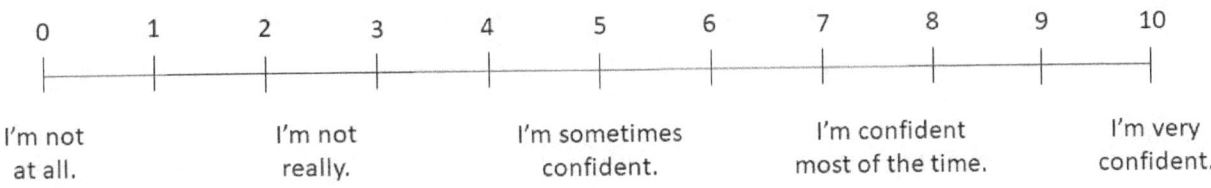

How confident are you in your ability to make productive choices in line with what you want in your work or career?

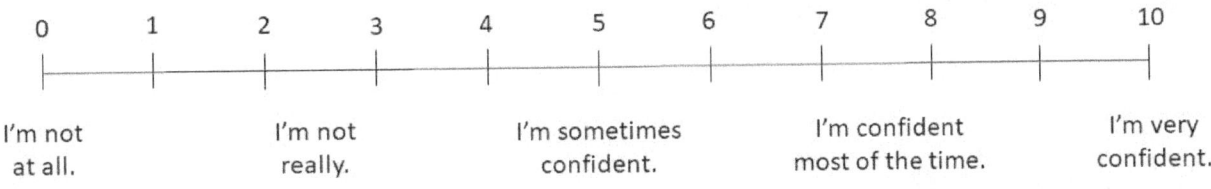

How confident are you in your mental strength to manage expectations of your work life balance?

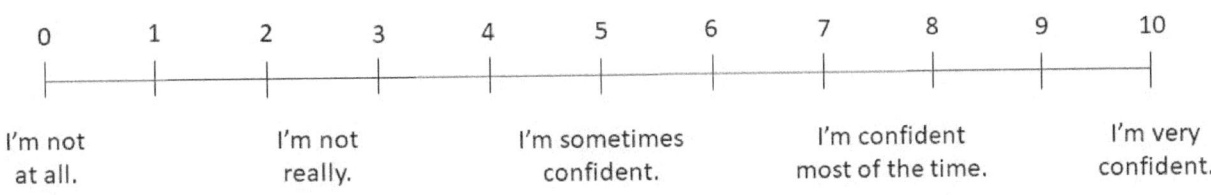

Scale Interpretation

Add up all your points.

0-35 – You may be overly critical of yourself, or you know that you really need to work on your confidence in your ability to organize your thoughts and make choices that are in line with your Personal Visions.

36-65 - You know that you really need to work on your confidence in your ability to organize your thoughts and make choices that are in line with your Personal Visions. You can do this!

66-105 – You are insightful and understand that sometimes you are confident and sometimes you are not. This is a great place to start. Everyone can use improvement!

106-140 - You are very confident in your ability to organize your thoughts; The Mentally STRONG Method can definitely help you improve even more!

141-170 – You are already well on your way to being able to organize your thoughts and make choices that are in line with your Personal Visions. If you had a perfect score though, I urge to look a little deeper. None of us are perfect and you may need to gain some insight into your thoughts and feelings.

What was your score? _____

Did you think that the scale is accurate? _____

Where would you like to be? _____

Never Give Up

My battle cry is **"Never Give Up!** I often repeat this phrase to myself; in fact, it has become the theme song of my life. I hope that it will become yours, too. Believe me when I tell you that I know that feeling of failure; I have experienced it before and have felt like a failure many times in my life. Today, I continue to experience that feeling on a regular basis, but I don't let it stop me. It doesn't define me.

I've set out to achieve many goals that have flopped. I've had to alter them because things change (that's life). At those times, I've had no choice but to adapt and adjust my plans. There are also many decisions that I've made along the way which I will forever feel were the wrong ones (but I don't beat myself up over them anymore).

Life events will occur that you didn't plan for; things you don't anticipate will happen despite vigilant planning. As you continue your journey with the Mentally STRONG Method, you will need to use this real-life practical formula over and over again to adjust and grow as your life ebbs and flows.

There is no magical solution to fix everything that's wrong in your life or to make everything instantly easier (if only there were). But you now have a way to take control. The Mentally STRONG Method is a process which empowers you to gain knowledge and insight about yourself so that you can build mental strength. You will use that strength to persevere through the good times *and the bad* (because both will be there along the way).

I can assure you that the use of the Mentally STRONG Method will be worth the hard work that you put into it. You will begin to understand yourself and how you make choices, decisions, and act in other areas of your life. I urge you to practice these newly gained Choice Mapping skills and take them with you on your continued journey through this real, complicated, messy LIFE. You will not regret it.

And, along the way, NEVER GIVE UP and always remember, you ARE Mentally STRONG!

"You have uncovered the ability to be Mentally STRONG. Choose perseverance in the journey."

- Dr. B